The
Great
Dimestore
Centennial

The
Great
Dimestore
Centennial

Don Byrd

BARRYTOWN, LTD.

STATION HILL

Published by Barrytown, Ltd. / Station Hill
in Barrytown, New York 12507.

E-mail: publishers@stationhill.org
Online catalogue: http://www.stationhill.org

Station Hill Arts is a project of The Institute for Publishing Arts, Inc., a not-for-profit, federally tax exempt organization in Barrytown, New York, which gratefully acknowledges ongoing support for its publishing program from the New York State Council on the Arts.

Designed by Susan Quasha.
Cover design by Susan Quasha and George Quasha with photographs by the author.
Drawings in Book IV and part title pages by Jondi Keane.

Library of Congress Cataloging-in-Publication Data

Byrd, Don, 1944-
        The great dimestore centennial / Don Byrd.
        p. cm.
        ISBN 1-58177-069-3 (alk. paper)
        I. Title.

    PS3552.Y666 G7 2001
    811'.54—dc21

                                                2001037721

Manufactured in the United States of America.

CONTENTS

FOR THE MANY AND THE MORE

The Great Dimestore Centennial is the prelude to *The Nomad's Encyclopedia*, a work in one-hundred volumes, which I propose to compile and publish. It is dedicated to the Third or Mutant Population which appeared as the *spiritual* consequence of increased levels of radioactivity in the 1940s.

God is not so limited as to need to repeat itself.

ACKNOWLEDGMENTS

In the following text I quote, and more often misquote, many other writers. My only defense against plagiarism is to say that I have appropriated their words but not their meanings. Readers will occasionally recognize words from famous writers, but here they have no more authority than Alice Morse Earle, Arthur C. Abbot, or the makers of texts who edit wire service copy for the Albany *Times-Union*. The meanings are all my own. The authority belongs to the poem.

The quotations which appear on the title page of each book are from the writings of Ludwig Wittgenstein.

This work was completed with the generous help of grants from The Creative Artists Public Service Project and the Research Foundation of the State University of New York. Thanks to Jondi Keane for drawings in Book VI, and on the seven part title pages.

Parts of the poem have previously appeared in *Credences*, *Adz*, *Hambone*, and *Wch Way*.

I might make a disclaimer similar to the one which appears on the title page of Arthur C. Abbot's amazing anatomy, *The Colors of Life*: The quality of materials used in the manufacture of this book is governed by continued postwar shortages.

THE GREAT DIMESTORE CENTENNIAL

It is apparent the so-called ten cent stores have contributed tremendously to a lower cost of living in making commonplace articles such as hardware, glass, and all the various things they sell in such quantities that useful and artistic objects have become widely distributed.

—T. W. Arnold

On my trip around the world I flew from west to east, and the whole Cinerama expedition proceeded in that way. But in the Seven Wonders of the World *on the screen it's around the world from east to west, the other way. Things are always getting turned around.*

—Lowell Thomas

THE BOOK OF THE MOON

Ask yourself: What would it be like if human beings never
found the word that was on the tip of their tongues.

I am the bearer of absolute knowledge, and this knowledge is, the moment I think, incarnated in one eagle. I am not only a thinking being, I am also—and above all—eagle.

I have nothing to hide. I'm writing a book, telling all. It's a cannibal. It's not inappropriate to laugh. If you laugh, the book will wait. It has perfect timing, and it will love you for your laughter.

If I were offered human flesh, at a party, would I eat it? Would I believe a morsel had stuck in my teeth and spend my life with a toothpick, trying to set this bit of human free? Thus, originating ethical speculation—a word, speculation, having to do with light, sight, and hiding in dry leaves.

I am suggesting that the apples on Eve's tree were people, growing in their natural states.

Enter the filose chronicle:

The tailor's posture at the writing desk,
the Hausfrau's posture,
for one and one add up here,
where painting comes to an end,
and canvasses are rolled up,
put away in odd-shaped
closets under the stairs, and stairs
come to an end. A time comes,
and the grid of possibilities is rolled up,
put away in a damp cellar.
Everything is known, the Way
and everything. The paths are rolled up
and put away in attics,
with old clothes and photographs—
false family histories in mementos,
cold spaces and collywobbles,
veiled to sleep, valed to sleep,
in the house in the vallium.

So tree diagrams let down
their dependencies. Yesterday

is installed in the Museum
of Ancient Arts and Instrumentalities.
Was it once? or the other:
it's an art of time,
solely. If the time be
improper, slow or wheezing,
the day will have been
no more than an instance,
exemplifying itself, but itself
is not itself, its time—
the dissonant reflexive,
contradictory nubbins, and laws requiring
bodies delivered to cemeteries
for cremation to be accompanied
with a certified statement
that the body contains
neither battery nor power cell.
The bell rings, the truck
makes its appointed rounds.
Eating a brown cow Marilyn
waits in her name—
an archaeological site.

All the Arts and Sciences convene
to think they might have
relieved her waiting—
that anyone might speak of One,
especially Marilyn. Even her name
comes in two, like ears,
Lolo, Lolo, without hearing,
equilibrium, the head
unfinished without ears—
no timbre in the thimble,
no hammer, no anvil,
no timber in the woodwinds,
no brass in the violins,
and words: surds—
their roots irrational.

He kept hearing the music,
he kept writing the song,
his mind kept changing itself
until it was a breeze
his friends heard as prophesy
and then it was a tortoise
in a fable.

Knowing is becoming
alienated from one's self,
Tomasso Campanella wrote,
becoming alienated from one's self
is going mad, losing one's own being
and assuming an alien being.

He has nothing to hide,
his hair is tied back to
uncover his ears. His ears
are shells—listen to them,
you will hear the sea.
In his eyes, you will see
yourself, if you are there;
if not, the wall behind
yourself, and the painting
on the wall.
It may be a scene of war,
she said, pulling the cap down
to cover her eyes,
or just a design, called here
The Entelechy of Music.
You like the red? Unjustly
your favorite color,
and I like green,
but yesterday I liked blue,
and it may be a shell:
listen—do you
hear the sea
               traffic
the last clock ticking.

We gave her stationery
for her birthday,
but it didn't work:
she died before she wrote
any letters.
The monogram
was a figure of the moon,
and the date was preprinted
because letters are all written
the same day and arrive
a week later.
The stamp is canceled,
the post box
rented to another patron,
and the PYEano is walking,
                            upstairs
it appears. It's stately, grand
and weighs as much as the Northwest Passage.
It speaks *The Moonlight Sonata*
in accents I might identify,
if the sky were quiet,
and I were eating baked beans
by the sisterly sea:
the religious belief therein,
the love and uncertainty.

You do this more than once't
and the train seeps outa
the sky,
           outa the sky and you do this
more than once't, so you die a little,
a litter of grave pups,
and you do this more than once't so
twice't awaitin'
for the (t)rain
soak't up a little by spongy clouds
bell ringing and tatting virgin
goddess (eyeing the nice man), Because
goddess who has not yet yet

                           yet returns
burnous of water,
                    burnous of fire,
each twenty-eight days.

The stroll and the amble are recursive gaits,
the gestures pictured in standard rhetorics likewise,
geometries of expression:
the twenty-eight parts of the model's face
allow one combination for each day of the year,
representing different facial expressions:
she turns her head
                   and spreads her legs.
She can be filled with water.
She is German? Yes.
Laughter (it says) marks a gain of lust.
What marketh song?
                In England

                         is Morse code
and the accompanying sign
a disguised bird;
in Germany, it's the opening of Beethoven's Fifth.
In Germany, it was disputed
whether an asparagus or the Madonna
was the more appropriate subject for art.
Proponents of asparagus won.
Ours is the age (it says) after Utopia,
in the theater where Franz Lizst conducted *Lohengrin*,
in the studio where *Name that Tune*
and *Your Hit Parade* were telecast.
Ours was the age after song:
consider this that.
That that that that sentence contains:
a Xosa girl went to the stream to draw water,
and there met with a member of the spirit world.
A member! That this:

Kibbo Kift, the Woodcraft Kindred,
the building of wigwams,
the playing of tom-toms,
repeating the same gestures,
responding to the same facial expressions,
moving to the same beat, this that.
That that that that that:
music has not improved since those late quartets
of Beethoven's,
                              dark with excessive brightness,
and their darkness is a death
that shines as we penetrate.
                                The qua-
stars (we hear)
                    that this that this this:
the sandwich board man
walks up and down the boardwalk.

Is this—asks an alien—an act of communication?
Perhaps. But wait:
the sandwich board man is an alien too.
He's a hired hand?
No! he doesn't understand the language.

What we hear of the quasars
may be the origin (roaring)
or near the origin, so far away.
And Beethoven was a sandwich board man.
His movements were jerky, his
gestures deformed. He spilled his inkwell
into the piano, and the piano was dark
in his excessive brightness.
                                He attempted
(O Lord!) he tried to write without themes,
to exploit energies locked within chords.
Musical information is located in memory,
in the left hemisphere for the musician
and the right hemisphere for the non-magician—
it establishes in our natures

rules of action:
some facet of the crystal here or there,
theres,
heres (hears) another facet dreaming,
the apotheosis of adorable Dutch tears—
the crystal drops of chandeliers.

Enter the filose chronicle,
so heavily interpreted the text itself disappears:

the French Revolution disappears;
the robots take tea with us, speaking of politics,
like astrobiologists,
                    like listening to Beethoven.

Deaf, deft with chopsticks,
their cursive clear and distinct in das *Gesprächenbuch,*
recursive, from ears to earwigs.
Earwigs
          have attained subsocial organization,
so have ambrosia beetles.
Why haven't we?
The embiids run forward and backward
with equal facility in their narrow homes.
Hereditary nobles were admitted
to the Bailiwick Assembly,
whether they possessed a fief or not,
a fife or not,
a knife, pillow cases
marked MASTER and SLAVE. (And do I, my dear,
get to sleep on the MASTER pillow tonight,
as if to lay my head on the moon?)
They have been called sexual guided missiles.
Male house flies have been observed courting
raisins (I too
have courted beings which proved to be
inanimate).
                    One orchid pollinates itself by exploiting

the sexual indiscriminativity of wasps;
nativity of orchids.
                              Parasite: mimesis
of the inorganic.

In the largo: a ghost;
the presto: eyes, almost grey
and blue, almost blue.
                              I liked your face.
I hope you survive its anger, your beauty—
you were going off to play pin ball,
a mirror image you peel off
and stick to your face, like pieces of tape,
the piecemeal effigy becomes you,
the lesions mark you,
                              Ephesian graces.
You are two and then more,
                              the Legions of Herostratus,
who burn the Artemision
the very night Alexander the Macedonian is born.
And the pin-ball game goes on,
though you are not playing.
The toilet is sweating: it works hard.

We pay dearly for civilization.
Civilization, it says: I do not sleep well
on the SLAVE pillow, the moon full,
and the mad wolves howling assassins tumbling
from Urgrund—
                              the time is now was,
later was
and now because even today,
even today
                              curvaceous nudes on sarcophagus lids
tempt the masculine hand to stroke it.
Even today: two and more times are now was new,
counting, measurement, and exact notation,
elaborate performances of leisure, jazz
(pronounced yats) and avant-garde sex,

translating *Alice in Wonderland* into Russian,
in the valley between the Great Wars.
The time is now:
                    bronze age war chariots
preceded farm wagons.
And why has laughter taken its actual form?
Why don't we wiggle our toes instead?
Instead,
            the hope of instant millennia
faded in the second and third centuries A.D.
Down in Boise City townspeople crowded
into the Palace Theater to see
Randolf Scott in *The Last Round Up*
before accepting the theory of outside invasion
ex abrupto.
            The time was now is was:
with a penny whistle,
as my consort plays a washboard—
tophat-totthratt-tophlatortratt—
Whew!
            takes a lot of penny whistles to play
a millennial tune.

Consider Dr. Samuel Tissot's three books:
on onanism (causes madness),
on the disorders of people of fashion,
on the diseases of literary and sedentary persons,
for which he prescribes nutmeg, cinnamon,
fennel, chervil, and walking.
                    Am I here speaking
of an alien?
                He was the physician Napoleon
engaged for his ailing mother.
And did he, with the aid of an aulos player,
quell the ravings of the mad young Tauromenan
by means of spondaic song?
The streets still had to be crossed on stilts.
A few wooden piles sunk in,
great stones brought in by boat,

a new district rose in the lagoon.
A substance in royal jelly promotes
the production of queens and may be regarded
historically as a single event—
evolution, learning, perception, hallucination,
and dreaming differing from one another only
in their time rates of change.
The time is now was changing rates of change.
A nation may overcome the disadvantage—
an excessive wealth of language,
a richness of heart and its natural concomitant,
a vast unfathomable deep of ideas,
a few wooden piles sunk in, to my knees
and rising, vast stones brought in by boat,
to my eyes ideas and rising, vast,
a new district arises in the lagoon,
and it may be overcome in two ways:
by distraction and addition,
machines of memory (lost) and illusion.
Von Neumann's machine builds other machines
from descriptions—descriptions of itself?
                              Descriptions
of itself and others.
                    In the course of electromagnetic
evolution, information and certainty
are brother and sister, perhaps incestuous.
Like Phillipe Ricord, the Voltaire of pelvic literature,
the parent machines (of memory and illusion) must
view its off-spring with suspicion.
Ricord would have submitted Artemis to treatment
with his mineral specifics and ordered
a course of blue pills for the vestal virgins.
The discomforts of Venus might be transmitted
throughout the robotic generations.
The gonococcus is as adaptable as the cockroach.

And what of the apparati which permit us
to quarter sensibility and draw it out
beyond this old body?

                            and is it possible?
Yes, yes, yes, yes,
                      is it possible?
without rendering the nervous system
into a state of uncontrollable oscillation.

The reformer hath enemies in all
who profiteth by the old order
and only luke-warm defenders in all
who profiteth by the new.
                            O! luke-warm defenders,
luke-warm defenders, uncontrollable oscillations,
who begin to nomadize, to stay in one place:
sneaking through brambles where grammars
join and run,
                  run, ready to travel—
disappear yes packed:

including
a rubber macintosh
tooth brush
galoshes
long johns
an old valise
including
infinite melody
a chain of stores
attracting new merchandise
soap
medicine
a Number 2 Kodak camera.

Infinite melody voices most sweetly the danger.

Enter the filose chronicle:

There appears to be a cellist in the band,
there appears to be some jello in his hand,

there tend to be many traffic
accidents on national holidays.
Schlesinger says, Americans should give up
the custom of drinking gas on the Fourth of July.
Heraclitus failed to account for the Volunteer
Fire Department.
                  Wilks said that whether one refers
to a single real process as hearing
or interpretation is a matter of taste,
and if Thorne gave no further hint
of the quarry he was pursuing,
he was doing no more than bringing Wittgenstein's
worries before a larger audience.
Thorne gave no hint, no sacred stone,
theophanic site (cite), no bethel
or priestly skin which served Jacob for a bed—
a drone state, an atmospheric oblivion,
a tin-magnesium-aluminum alloy,
developed by Minneapolis-Honeywell
repairs its own breaks:
                  a quarter
of the universe transformed itself,
                            hydrogen to helium—
the first twenty-minutes of cosmic evolution.
The interstellar clouds are too hot, too
magnetic,
              they rotate too rapidly,
they repair their own breaks:
they do not simply become stars
                      or honey
or Minneapolis.

Our galaxy formed fifteen billion years ago,
as a gaseous cloud.
The first generation of stars appeared thereafter.
And did Wittgenstein worry?
And did the wider audience share his worries?
He worried;
            they shared.

The spherical galaxy collapsed,
extending long spiral tentacles.
Orbiting from one arm to another,
the clouds were passed along (they
had nothing better to do),
and Beethoven took rooms at 1081 Walfishgasse,
which he knew to house a brothel.
During the passage the densest,
coldest part of the cloud
passed the point of no return and collapsed.
Discos of dust,

            which he knew to house a brothel,
orbited the star.
What made the discs of dust divide into rings?
and what caused the rings to transform into planets?
This is the most obscure part of the story.
A large body swept by earth,
was broken by tidal forces, worried
stretched out like a panatela,
and sly earth captured some part of it.
Lunar inscription entered a drone state,
an atmospheric oblivion.
No, this is the most obscure part of the story:
the child sits in bed, motionless, smiling,
apparently friendly,
she sometimes laughs,
claps her hands, she does not rock.
She plays with cubes and toy people.
She is content
to repeat stereotyped gestures,
usually moving these objects in circles.
She does not rock,

            she does not rock,
she repairs her own breaks.
The first crystal is a nucleus, the process
nucleation,

         atoms arranged in three-dimensional
patterns —

        lattices, like tragedies or minds.

A dislocation perpendicular to the Burger's vector
is an edge; parallel is a screw—
the influence of thermal agitation,
perhaps from hot springs and volcanoes,
the vocabulary made-up of three-letter words
(and no exclamation points):
the physical features little more than hieroglyphs.
There are no exclamation points in genetics.

The volume and surface area of a body
do not expand together:
                                    animals grow larger,
risk asphyxiating themselves with their own bulk.
The amphibian is not a distant relative
Brother Salamander—
we belong to the same subphylum.
Ritual cannibalism at Chou Kou Tein
500,000 years ago.
                            Homo sapiens replaced
classic Neanderthal man—
                                    an interglacial period.
They had no organized men's houses, hardly
practiced some orgiastic dances,
blood vengeance and so forth: the folklore
of the times, called today law,
                                    economics,
bit by bit the organic matter leached out,
atom by atom replaced by synthetic substitutes—
it does not rock.
It returns to chaos to orgy
to dark water.
When the seven planets assemble
in Cancer, there will be deluge;
when they meet in Capricorn, there will be drought.
These circuitous paths to death,
faithfully followed by the conservative instincts,
would thus present us with the picture of
the phenomenon of human life:
she wakes him up,

to keep him from sleeping, to keep him there,
in the room, in the bed,
like god in the tabernacle.
These gestures acquire meaning
(it says)
       solely to the extent they repeat
primordial acts.

Errors were made
at the Ceremony of Life: errors, pallor, cyanosis,
songs of life sung in deathly meters,
and you have entered the space where
appearances are generated.
You have a dragon tooth in your ear lobe,
and you cannot go back whence you came
because the path too is an appearance
which leads to Memphis, and Memphis
is a disappearance,
          though you might
go by steamboat to Cairo (in Illinois)
and by bus thence to Paducah,
which is a nice town with a park.
You might decide to settle down there—
people have chosen less attractive places.
You might attain local notoriety
as the Tooth of Paducah.
         There's room
for a few more operators,
and you should speak to Herman
at the Appearance and Reality Pool Room:
he's the only man in the South,
who can put four pool balls in his mouth,
or appear to.
You and he might team up—
do some theater of the most philosophic kind
(which is not THE-ayter at all),
and then. . . .

Then enter the filose chronicle,
so interrupted the next itself appears:

Mao shaved his queue;
the rebels painted their eyebrows red;
they wore yellow turbans;
they climbed snow-covered mountains, ate rocks,
slept in snow, marched and fought,
and marched again.
                              Mao wrote *On Protracted War*,
ignoring food, sleep, for nine days—
on the seventh day failed to notice the fire
burning a hole in his left shoe.
He worked the marble at right-angles,
taking care no part of the figure be left behind:
a square or rectangular face,
a red bulb in the middle of the forehead,
big nose, long ears, protuberant,
frog-like eyes,
his face was putty-color.
He seemed to fly
in a green suit, with shining buttons,
in a green tam-o-shanter, in Coldwater, Kansas.

Am I speaking here of an alien?
                              Probably.
It takes a lot of voices to sing a millennial song.
The Bach is guitar transcribed for rain.
I try to beat the moon out of a vision.
The rain is Bach transcribed for guitar.
I try to beat a vision out of the moon.
The guitar is rain transcribed for Bach.
I try to vision a moon out of the beat.

At this stage in our investigation we must
guard against a circular movement, a circular
movement of the heart:
                              I can play chess naked,

but I can't concentrate, I can't concentrate.
The scene of the crime too is deserted.
It is photographed for the purpose
of establishing evidence.
In fact, if we want to be exact,
we do use a gesture or a facial expression.
It takes a lot of faces to sing a millennial song.
It takes a lot of attention if the pure
scientist is a schiz,
                        if the pure artist,
reading in bed, crams sheets into his mouth
to stay the excitement, if we don't have time
but quite the reverse: the begonia blossom
just dries and drops off, and the hysterical music
on the radio finally weeps,
because the mind is an ancient Greek idea.
Uttering a word is like striking a note
on the keyboard of the imagination:
                            in Cuba,
a vagina is a papaya, believe me,
a papaya.
        The Corsican guerillas sang
Jerusalem Delivered (Tasso), believe me,
and the French developed techniques for turning
church bells into guns,
to try a new town,
to expand,
            to think in a big territorial way.
Since expansion is everything,
                            I'd annex the planets,
Cecil Rhodes said,
                allowing those capable
of *in vitro* clonal growth to form colonies
and bridges between galaxies,
the capture of material from one galaxy
by another.
                    Another by
galaxy one from material of capture the
galaxies between bridges and

draw it out over this new body—
its nervous system in uncontrollable oscillation.

If a Chinese merchant bought twenty
yards of cloth he would buy seven-hundred and twenty
    inches,
but when he sold it he would sell it by a short yard—
a yard
        might be twenty-four inches long.
Your foolsworth in the timestore:
Frank Woolworth wanted to sell a watch
for a dime, a good watch. Life's
more than engineering: one thinks also,
one thinks, two thinks. Yard-goods,
hardware, carrot peelers, and school supplies,
an egg-timer, calibrated, opinionated—

        A Squishy Egg
        THE PERFECT EGG
                (The Harvest Moon)
        A Rubbery Egg—

handles for hot ears of corn
and bug-eyed gold fish (your malefic spirits
will not enter so hopeless a creature). Croesus,
whose army sacked the Artemision,
presented the columns required for its restoration
and some cows of gold (or cows which shat
gold).
        The posh
57th Street galleries right next door to Sak's
Fifth Avenue and Bonwit
Teller. Some comrades
forgetting we were in swamp, would run
head-long into mire.
                        Ho-lung's wife
gave birth on the march.
Kang Ke-ching, wife of Chu Teh

carried weapons and wounded soldiers.
Mao laughed until he wept
at a description of *Modern Times*
(Chaplin).
The Long March was a manifesto,
three times longer than Xenophon's,
and Mao's chief luxury was a mosquito net,
and the Long March was a seeding machine,
but this was the land of the dreaded Lolos—
the tribal horns calling men to battle,
WUNG-G-G-G, WUNG-G-G-G,
WUNG-G-G-G-G.

I live on a houseboat called China,
she lives in a boathouse called China,
too hot to sleep, too hot to sleep, too hot to sleep,
to read a thousand books, a thousand and one books:
there I did it again, I did it again,
riding the cat right through the storm: meatus,
bowels, sentences—
one would think after a while
I would learn,
I would harden myself,
especially my heart:
from this oddly specific muscle,
one-way valves in the veins of arms, legs—
love a stricter discipline than poetry.
Orpheus did not build temples
in their hearing; he created ears
as anaclitic objects.

Aprés Vu:
I'm going to see this again,
assassination by metaphysics, one case
(unconfirmed).
The English terrorist, Bishop Berkeley,
snuffed out Nicholas Malebranche.

Houston said,
I'm going to see this again:
Profit squeezes have forced many dealers
to trim their services, lay off
employees and sacrifice personal moral standards
to survive.
Dallas said, I find all the things
that are Thursday:
                         the colors of tradesmen are mostly dry
as when the grass withers—red
as when it burns away.
I start with the sense
that justice is next to the nebulous thing
I cannot describe:
                         your synthetics will be very hot,
materials like polyester knits and nylons.
They are just not absorbent,
and they don't allow your body to breathe.
They just hold the moisture in
and that is why you become clammy
(especially your heart).
Morrison said: There is great possibility
some form of intelligent life exists in the universe
(and they won't allow your body to breathe),
but he added that Congress has refused
to fund a $14 million project that would search
for radio waves.

Having made one argument,
without removing my hat,
I'll make another:
It might be a friendly abyss.

Enter the filose chronicle because,
because the philose chronicle,
and because

         The ancient tales cannot be doubted:
         A dragon guards the treasure—

Presumably gold, jewels and gold.
The dragon sleeps in measure.

The old stories tell us
Those who stray from their grammar
Go where dragons sleep
And witches clamor.

From these haunted, speechless places,
Language witches wink and smile,
Counting steps through endless spaces
Until you face the wymre and trial,

And if you bed the witch with pleasure,
Counting strokes and keeping measure,
You will find in her mild eyes
Dim floating figures of paradise,
But if in frenzy you lose the number,
You disturb the dragon's slumber,
And against his plated scales,
Mad majestic terror fails.

Because every star spends its life in struggle
against gravity.
Every atom in the sun
is attracted to the center.
One thousand solar masses
is sufficient to crush the magnetic field
which threads through it.
                              In these towns
I've seen fresh corpses,
shallow graves also of famine and disease,
and rich men there, rice hoarders,
wheat hoarders, money lenders,
diseases of love:
the infecting spirochete—
a corkscrew spiraling organism—
penetrates the skin or mucous membrane;

scurvy came into its own with the great sea voyages;
pellagra in the eighteenth century;
beriberi in Asia;
the attitude of the U.S. Cavalry
in Dakota was more determined by the deep
structure (the more determined) than the surface
structure of the sentences;
in the fifth month, she said,
                                        my father died;
in the sixth I developed a rash;
in the ninth I burned my back
and shoulders with cleaning fluid;
one week before delivery a car I was riding in
was struck by another car.

As for that man he died
                                (her father);
as for this woman she was pregnant
itchy, burned, struck;
as for the child her breath smelled,
sometimes he had a chocolaty complexion,
and then her breath smelled worse.
She did not rock. As for this,
it is an analog computer, not a vending machine.
Some actions required of the machine—
kissing and weeping—are not possible.
The poet supplies a description,
gesture supplies the rest,
and the wrong pitch on one syllable
can change the meaning:
From the waves once more I see the calm
becomes Once more I see a cat
coming from the waves.
The stimulus is registered by image demons,
analyzed by feature demons
(nomads thrive in these areas).
They give the syllable the wrong pitch:
think of buns growing from the side of bread,
broken eggs in shoes and Christmas trees

decorated with mustard,
a small platform of green schist,
with a sacred tree and an altar,
                              a goddess
with many breasts and swathed below the waist
with grave cloths—the epiphenomenal thighs
and their delights—red clay gumbo sticky,
sticks to the boots.

Nomads rotate between these areas
and two-hundred years of drought.

As for the Ephesians, they twice supported
the unsuccessful party, gave shelter
first to Brutus and Cassius and afterwards
to Anthony.

Thereafter Ephesus seems to have been deserted,
owing to miasmic air and supporting
the unsuccessful party.

The trio's oxygen tank exploded enroute,
transforming the command capsule—Lovell said—
into a tomb.
Water was in short supply,
and the astronauts discovered they couldn't
jettison their urine
                    for lack of power.
Thereafter desert peoples began
to use dromedaries;
thereafter desert peoples began to use Cadillacs:
Mesopotamian artifacts in Harappa
and Mohenjo-Daro on the Indus;
amazonite beads from the Nilgiri Hills
in the flood silt of Ur.
Deserts were reported to be on the march.
Nomads rotate between these pockets of unrest—
my hands in pockets of unrest.

The picts pressed on Hadrian's wall.
Shapur I proclaimed himself King of Iran
and non-Iran. Mickey Rooney
played Puck in Hollywood Bowl.
The nomads rotate between these areas,
fastening on eye-catching snippets
from the inherited body of learning,
black blizzards and sand blows,
                              brown earth
from Montana and Wyoming swirled up,
was captured by high-level winds
and blown eastward: Dubuque by late afternoon,
Chicago by evening,
Buffalo the following midday—
a sharp peppery smell,
                    a nauseating greasiness
doth keel the pot.
                    Gothic tribes
moved first into the land around the Vistula,
and thence, through southern Poland, to the Black Sea;
the Ostrogoths settled in the Ukraine;
the Visigoths occupied a wide region,
eastward from the lower Danube;
the Quadi threatened the frontiers
from Carnuntum to Regina Castrum;
the Franks absorbed the Saxons
of the Elbe and the Weser.
The English and Turks call it the French disease;
the Persians blame it on the Turks;
the Flemish and Dutch refer to it as the Spanish pox;
the Spanish call it the disease of Española,
where Columbus had been;
the Russians think of it as a Polish ailment.
Most organisms reproduce asexually,
but retain the option of gene-mixing
every tenth or hundredth or thousandth generation,
to stir the mix anew.

Artemis herself put the capstone on the temple.
She came to the desperate architect in a dream.

When he woke the impossible stone was lifted,
but she has failed rapidly of late.
The accustomed glance of her lovers
no longer animates her image of herself,
revives her faded photograph.

Ernest says she may drop away any time.

Outer eye, overt *lettre de cachet*, gulls.
If this be a coastal city, if it be washed
but not washed out, the outer eye is the sea
or near the sea, and its birds are common.
When the weather permits it, they are rash
and sashay across the strand as if they own it.
If you stand by the window by the sea,
if the weather be fair enough—O! weather be fair
enough—and if the window is open, the air
itself is a message. That is one kind of day
and one kind of bird. The message is air and sea.

Outer eye, overt *lettre de cachet*, pelicans.
If this be the ultimate coast and coastline
of man, the outer eye is nearer the sea
or the sea is larger, and its birds are odd,
skillful in the tasks of their lives,
singular in their vertical competence.
There are no windows, no windows by the sea,
and the weather is fair—some say too fair,
though they are mistaken—and I am the window,
and the window is the message on this day,
watching the pelicans. A message watches the window.

The bird of the inner eye is a bird of circumspection.
It is red, orange and red, assertive, neither a city
nor near a city. It is a place which leaves itself.
The migratory eye dishes itself out, out of itself,
out of itself. It is the inner flight of birds
out of themselves, when the weather demands it,

and if the weather be fair enough—O! be it—
the inner bird sings, and it sings at a window
it never sees, this red bird of the monad,
itself a message, but not the only message, red
and aching with love. The message opens a window.

Little known bird of the inner eye is a quadruped.
If this be the ultimate interior, the outer is nearer,
goes into itself, where the red is understood
as the grammar of desire, which reduplicates its radical,
as in Nootka: *Hluch*—'woman'—forms *Hluchluch-ituhl*
'to dream of a woman,' and *Hluchluch-k'ok*—
'resembling a woman,' and the bird bird
of love love singes sweetes songes in mine ear.
The message is the window of the window,
and if the window is air I will fly there,
there, where a message of flight resembles a woman.

THE BOOK OF THE GARDEN

Language is a labyrinth of paths. You approach from one side and know your way about; you approach the same place from another side and no longer know your way about.

```
PRAK        A                    KRET
   E     SWERBH G  S              E
   W   B E        W  T     B      W
BHERDH I         E  E     H    KLENG
   H    E PLEU    R  N     ERKW     H
AR      D  E      PEYE     I    E    E
   E   BHREUS    R            G  R    R
   G    H   D  AIW   DEIW    PLEK
   R    E  BHREN E   H          E
   E AL       E  R   E       SNEIT
   W  G     G    DHENG  W  G    G
BHENDH    DHENGH    H   E       H
H         R      KWER  I     GER
E         KEU     E  L   DHABH E
G      S  A     DEU          T  E B
   D  SWEN      H            E  N H
 BHER  E        E           GHER D
   E    I    KAN   O   H
DEL WENDH    E      B   R
E G E      GENE   H  KEU
I   I       E      E  A      HERE
KWERP       R     GLEUBH
```

*The Garden of
Indo-European Roots*

*to live and breathe
to shine
to turn
to bind*

The seeds
of flowering plants
show
two sheaths—
leaves
which form
and protect
the young plant
presently turning
to the light.

In higher
animals

fertilized eggs
form
outer sheaths
by which
containers
of the body
are shut off
from the mother's
body
and the rest
of the world:

this is a Garden.

This is a garden, and now Her mastery, Earth's
settles as dust on living women, lines as true
as Mondrian's bow out to receive the content,
and I am uncertain how to accent *con*tent,
and I am uncertain how to accent con*tent*
or if I should take her by the hand, but I will,
or she will take her hand for me
(she always does), Great Sister of the Flaming
Kiss and Perfect Bowels, the desert contending
with art in the memory of teenage girls.

diggadigga
diggadiggadigga

Sad-eyed Sally Ellis—hidden source—resembled the mountain
love of Nebuchadnezzar, and Sal had a scar like a snake crawling
from her left shoulder into a neckline so low the chaperons turned us
away at the door to the Senior Prom. She resembled Cleopatra also,
the asp forever fixed at her breast.

Throwing petals from her gardenia corsage and my pink carnation
to the winds, we drove my yellow and black '52 Buick to the
Forestry Service fire tower south of town (this is the pastoral sym-
phony).

The moon was a neat, clear crescent, and we climbed the tower to be near it. I lied about the stars, inventing constellations and stories about them. This is the origin of civilization. I quoted The Hollow Men, The Second Coming, and two-thirds of Hymn to Intellectual Beauty. I shrieked and clasped my hands in ecstasy—I broke down laughing. This is the origin of civilization.

By then there were a dozen cars around the Tower, all radios tuned to Dick Meandi, WLS, clear-channel from Chicago, and Mary Jeanne jumped from the white Ford next to us, took three long steps and puked on my car. Dennis climbed the tower, saying he was going to jump. Mary Jeanne pukes every time I get my hand in her pants, whether she has been drinking or not. She's puked twice in my car. I'm going to jump: I can't stand the smell.

I recited The Hollow Men. Dirty Mike sang Love Me Tender, wriggling his ass like Elvis. Possum Stultz filled a condom with beer, threw it at Mike, and goosed Kay Ellen, who screamed and asked Hank Gillette, the banker's son, to take her home, but Suzanne had passed out in the back seat of Hank's T- bird. He had to sober her up.

Dirty Mike was transformed Great Balls of Fire into Jerry Lee Lewis.

Sal and I were finishing the rum BJ had procured for me in lieu of twelve bucks I'd won at snooker. Which should I be, Sal, a poet or a hustler? A poet or a hustler. I shoot pretty good pool, you know. What do you think? As Sal thought about my question, Dennis was screaming from the tower he would jump, Suzanne was moaning guilt and curses from Hank's car, and Tommy Creech made a crack about our being barred from the prom.

You apologize to Sal, I said, or I'll stick this rum bottle up your slimey ass as soon as we finish with it.

But Sal, squinting into the headlights of a leaving car crooked her right forefinger at me. Come here my giggling Shelley, she said.

yipyipyipyip
yipyipyipyip
boomboomboomboom
getajob:

Which I did, picking strawberries (my first
job), and they were ripe, turning my fingers
blood red, and my mouth and my fingers
were covered with bits of their flesh,
which was sweet. Culture
sustains itself with human
sacrifice.

Yipyipyipyip:
tsav, power
from eating human
flesh, and making gardens, scenes
of privileged moments when
self takes title
to itself (as a garden,
a strawberry in a garden, an art,
an artifact in a museum, a tree
in Central Park, a cultish ritual).
Babylon's reputation for wickedness, Jed said,
a result of its practice of ornamental
gardening, the refuge of nostalgiacs,
dogmatoids, and metaphysical engineers.
America's reputation for its practice
of intensive farming?
I am eating nitrogen fertilizer.
I am eating a steer,
the flesh of which is puffy.
All produce
can be specified now as puffy.
The Flaming Kiss does not come to the puffy gardener.
The puffy garden repeats itself. Confounded—
Babylon, America. Confounded great nations,
which exist between earth and mid-heaven

(where you arrive by ritual recirculation,
if you arrive, and time runs both directions,
if it runs). Gardens are lies to time.

Yipyipyipyipyip

I play a queer harmonica:
this is a garden.
George Gershwin and Cole Porter,
the history of popular music,
coming apart in my hands,
more fungi than flowers—what's this?
The object is not still,
still not still—it's slow
earth's laughing. The seismograph
gets the joke, records the laughter.
The coastlines of three continents are now
unknown, the name of the Mediterranean
is changed, being no longer appropriate;
the United States
are now dispersed,
and a charged circle of chords
takes flight.
Yesterday's
no storage problem—
it's light and portable.
The habits are here, hair
growing on your head. Your heart
keeps your hair growing; no!
your teeth shining, lining
the avenues of dying elms.
This is a garden (of dying elms),
hardened edges, hedges of privet,
boxwood, privacy, never more lonely
than in a garden or the thought
of a garden, a perspective of elms
to the vanishing point, and you are
vanishing to those who stroll
far down the erotic ratios of space.

O! stand back, the metaphysical
engineer, name of Nebuchadnezzar,
is in love with a country girl:
he'll build a garden (hanging),
and Tom Jefferson is a metaphysical
Adam—that is, he is not really
Adam, and the garden's a paradox,
more logical transgression than
bean rows. What's this?
—*My Country Tis of Thee*, in Debussy?
Les Préludes (to what? pray tell, I scream,
I scream, I scream, I scream.
I am a barbershop quartet,
she is a pilgrime,
we are sweet land, together).
The Hanging Gardens of Babylon,
the family farm: grain
hand raked from reaper platform,
hand bound, hand stacked,
hand pitched to bundle racks,
hand pitched to stack,
hand stacked, hand pitched to feeder platform,
hand fed to the threshing machine—
nine handlings,
                three of them stoop jobs—
the garden, the 1880s.
                And Babylon,
Babylon, Babylon,
in my words and a little to the left,
in Broca's area, in the garden of speech:
the evergreens are red, the bluebells are red—
a wondrous land, a reliable and noise-free indicator,
like writing, striking gestures, toothy smiles,
like a cabinet of psychic piano rolls.
We distinguish several hundred thousand
chromatic sensations (perhaps millions):
a portfolio of my desires.

My hands are hungry, summaries
of gestures, hunger

in the air, like a fog or a smell
(of a garden). The tender stars have eaten
only themselves; they are polite.
Red giants engage in self-denial more
absolute than any saint.
Perhaps they give up, as men do in the cold.
The cold is a friendly dog and licks your face.
You lie down as it comes and goes away,
carrying your child, who is raised by wolves.
When she is found—an adolescent—
she cannot learn human ways,
but humans can learn wolves' ways
(Babylon). She becomes a great teacher,
and when she retires her students
publish a *festschrift* in her honor.

I will have my fantasy about hands.
We will sing the song about tulips later,
after we've eaten,

                when our hands are satisfied,
when the gestures are true.
We will walk in the garden,

                    walking through fire,
reading the newspaper:
a figure may be a ghost by the gazebo;
a ghost may be a figure by the gazebo;
the logomorphs multiplying like rabbits;
the lagomorphs multiplying like habits.
Like pulling a wishbone, language squeals
before it breaks and the fire descendeth.
The northern lights are seen in this garden.
The displays take the form of arcs, rays,
bands, curtains, draperies,
coronas, and diffused glows,
accompanied by soft crackling sound,
like rustling silk,
or competition of two species
for the same prey,
like men and wolves.

The engineer's lady was oppressed by the low,
sandy plains of the fertile crescent.
It might be the moon, she said.
No mountain breeze cools my mountain
need. And Nebuchadnezzar took pity upon her.
Love's equal in length and breath
to the world (it says).
The garden is a semblance,
the birth of public works,
irrational fantasy invading the bee-hive complex,
the people, the invisible machine,
when replication of the world becomes so adequate,
it includes the replication; the replication,
it includes the replication.
A garden circular in plan,
concentric in organization,
centered on Babylon, not so much a place
as a series of vowels—
Babylon—encircled by Humiditas,
the province of whores,
those who sell their tongues
and the dew from their words
(a soggy swamp, a lexicon),
and again encircled by desert,
rich in thorns,
the dwelling place of virgins,
a digressive landscape,
confusing images of darkness and sleep
with waking life, misleading hallucinations,
disordered memories, unaccountable impulses.
The garden of Love does not contain itself:
this is the truest thing I can say,
not so much a place as a series of vowels
(a song). The singer of songs sings of
a singer of songs who sings a song
which is the song he is singing.
This song: I am not calling,
I am crossing (in song)
into new territory. An instinct
is an urge to restore an earlier

state—an urge to cross again.
Then we shall be compelled to say
(it says here, in this book,
Herr Freud's book), Death,
death is the aim of life.
That's the gardener's view, the landscape
of the agricultural mind, sloping
toward death. Hence arises the paradox:
the organism struggles against dangers
which promote quick attainment of the aim.

We wait to be choked by the by-
products of metabolism.

Wild plants in careful plots
swell at root or burgeon
with edible beans, aromatic seeds,
juicy flesh, and colorful flowers.
Identification of blood
and other manifestations of life—
the gardener's empiric knowledge
that to produce lusty plants
a hundred (including this one)
must be rooted out. But the singer
roots himself out?

The garden is a Dis

semblance:
like begats like less like
until more garden forestalls less likeness:
an ever presence of her absence,
the reverent absence of her referent,
a preference for her ever referent,
and the ab of my presence refers to her ever,
the pres of her reference is never absent,
her earth is present as her absence infers,
her flesh is ever and never present,

a circular motion is her preference,
pale leaves of boxwood, pale willows,
yellow and brown:
its brownness and dryness are present.
The Hanging Garden is gone,
didn't last a season
without the slave's water.
The Philosopher's Garden is gone
(Medici at Fiesole) and the water organs,
though the Romantic tradition persists
and like plantain spreads wherever the white man travels
(for example: names of suburban developments),
and landscape architects have tried
to reconcile the literary Arcadia
with Scarsdale, Winetka, and Overland Park.

I have not written as I wished,
by moonlight, Miss Earle says,
and I have written too much by it?

Too much:
consider the resemblance between respiration
and combustion. We have energetic hearts
and rapaciously absorptive blood.
This is a garden: the dynamic rush
and overall instability of the *milieu interior*.
A sprig of rue was given me
and chanced to lie with this writing paper
for a single night. The scent has never left it.
The odor of rue hangs about the whole book.
Thus, how pervasive a metaphor can be,
how persuasive a metaphor:
the living body cellularity is more than weave,
texture, grain.
Life uses left-handed amino acids
and right-handed sugars:
entwined strands, sugar-phosphate backbones,
bases projecting inward from the sugar moiety,
writing. The DNA double helix inscribes

three kinds of RNA's
forth to cytoplasmic history:
a chaos of unpersonalized feeling,
sporting and finding the germ
of a generalizing tendency—
an imperfection that takes form, a habit,
a habit that grows, a fifty-dollar-a-day habit.
The regularities of the cosmos evolve
until it is a perfect, rational,
symmetrical habit and mind crystalizes at last:
the semi-conductor, the imperfection of silicon,
the habit: electromagnetic
evolution. This is a garden.
Junkies gibbering in the park like pigeons.
Their habit is habit. In transistor theory,
it's said that holes—
places where electrons *might be*—flow.

I have seen snowing edgings of candy-tuft
and sweet alyssum. I should be loath
to use moneywort as an edging.
If it thrived well enough to make a close,
suitable hedge, it would thrive too well
and swamp the border. Thrift has been used as an edging
since the days of the old herbalist, Gerarde.

The common repetition of paradigmatic gestures,
as ways of measure,
as revealed ontology:
Linnaeus reads his floral clock,
blossoms opening and closing during the day.
The usual sequence in concentrated industry:
market control through collusion,
conspiracy, and cartels,
to non-price competition
ologopolistic interdependence.
And before clocks were invented, a monk
called his comrades to nightly prayers:
he began reading at dark;

when he reached a certain page in the book,
he'd ring the bell.
                    The book called

    Y?
    How do you make a Y?
    Something like a foot,
       right?

The monk something like a clock.
Ring the bell. TRNA
is central to the coding process:
it couples with an amino acid
and brings it into position,
in an excited state,
so it can react with other
amino acids to form protein,
in an excited state.

The anti-code, therefore,
seems to have preceded the code in evolution.
Having addressed the multitudes, he was
the multitudes; they were his memory.
The flow, the break-down, the mess
in the message: the anti-code first,
where the desert and the garden
strive for mastery, and the rock compelled
to yield the fig, the citron, and the orange,
to blossom with the myrtle and the rose.
This ignorance demands our clearest attention.
The Philosopher's Garden is gone,
and Cygnus X-l is trying to expand further.
As it moves into the red giant stage,
its companion gobbles up its outer atmosphere.
Space plotted horizontally,
time moves generally upward. So:
if undaunted, you look into the shaded region,
it is possible to avoid infinite forces
by following these trajectories
into another universe.

Parson Mather gives tansy and caraway as
remedies for hiccoughs; I prefer dill.
I prefer the French interpretation of symptoms—
their national fantasy about the liver—
to the English obsession with bowels.

Difficult to say where you feel
nausea or where to locate
the galloping mules of greed,
deep leviathans of lechery,
sickly worms of grief.
A number of rhythmic systems,
including hamsters (running activity),
neurospora (growth rhythms),
drosophila (leaf movements),
have been maintained at the South Pole,
a turn-table arranged to rotate counter
to earthly rotation, and they kept time.
The mules galloped.
It is said that whales beach themselves
because of the intolerable noise of the seas,
and grief recurs—difficult
to say where you feel earthly rotation.

I saw an aircraft involved in flames.
Two subjects were running away. The object
inside the plane was Thurman Munson.

 As light fails
red disappears
first
and appears black
while blues and
violets appear
bright
and greens
become grey.

This is an elegy for Thurman Munson
(though its boundaries are unclear).
Geometry is gone now.
The circumference of a circle
divided by its diameter is an irrational number,
an irrational number, in an excited state.
The earlier temples, grottoes and pyramids
have been removed (involved in flame).
Certain hard stones—flint, obsidian—
shatter to leave sharp edges
(leaves of glass),
but nearer Cleveland nights are longer.

The body is not stone, it is fire,
a voice speaking in fire—
the willingness of syntax to thicken,
hedgerows and borders of the hypogenetic empire.
The elegaic mood spills
beyond its boundaries.
I should be loath to use
moneywort as an edging;
I should not care
for its yellow flowers in that place,
though I find them cheerful
and kindly on dull banks or in damp spots—
the drips of trees and eaves.
I should be loath to follow the modern fashion
of pulling down walls and fences,
removing the boundaries of lawns,
and living in full-view of passers-by,
but no hedge thrives in the elegaic atmosphere.
O! the luscious dialectic of two
tongues in my mouth, mine
and yours, precise, sweet Alice,
my sublated transcendentalist guide
to the gardens, and Epsilon Aurigae
is a star much worth discussing,
one of the strangest in the sky,
whether it contains a black hole or not.

To get through the worm-hole,
into the anti-cosmos, you would
travel faster than light, you would:
hands, like lizards, green lizards,
with blue heads.

If what I am proposing here is true,
am I then pulling the cosmic trigger?
Can you walk like a puppet?

PULL THE TRIGGER,
welcome the aliens to our humble home.

As the tradition requires,
jets leave for Dallas and Singapore,
they leave for the anti-cosmos.
The aliens appear.

I have an opinion of Dallas,
though I have never been there:
the consolation of philosophy.
Would I know an alien,
if I saw one? Dallas
has undertaken
to replicate the Hanging Gardens
in plastic, though high-quality plastic:
two hundred variant leaves on the boxwood
alone, some yellowed or misformed.
And the women of Singapore
have the gift of smiling.
Their teeth are not white,
but they give
the impression of being.
If I were to go there,
I would buy a ring and give it
to a woman I met on the street.
I would tell her I liked her teeth,

and she would say,
That's not what you mean,
and she might be right,
but I don't think so.

Nebuchadnezzar is a shadowy figure:
let Carmine Galante stand in his place,
in New York instead of Babylon.
Galante was 5 foot 4—
a shadow in a floppy hat.
He had a cigar clenched in his teeth
the moment he died:
typical, the cigar.
Human flesh (in Tanna) is called long pig.
Protein may be a makeshift material—
it happened to be around.
Life, anyway, is not protein,
but music written on it,
a rhythm or riff
in the laws of thermodynamics.
Successively presented images
cease to be separate:
four strokes per second
on a snail's belly compels it to crawl,
to crawl upon a non-existent
surface, which it perceives as coherent,
and once an idea catches on, it
replicates itself,
non-physical genes, abstract DNA.

Galante kept a garden.
There he liked to grow tomatoes
and other vegetables.
Brutality was his trademark.

Can you walk like a puppet?

What if the nearest civilization is
in Sirius and keeps an eye on us?

Their signals are bound to dribble forth
into our digressive landscape,
among broccoli-like trees,
conclusions and beginnings flowing together
with caesura, linked by continuous gardens,
where one man in the company wears a floppy hat
and bears a great falcon on his gloved hand—
a verdant garden given over
to music-making ladies and playful dogs.
Parts of an exposition of death
and Last Judgment. Lovers
gathered in the Garden have little to do:
chin-chucking disappears—the fifteenth-century
Garden of Love, like the twentieth-century atom,
like wireless sets built of bamboo
and vines to keep in touch with Americans
and other spirits;
invasions in the form of viral
and bacterial infections,
drifting down from meteoric materials and comets—
comets expelled from stars
in their overluminous enthusiasm,
signs of celestial sex.

This is a garden.

An angry, joyous scream approximating a breath,
an excess of color as cloying
as its surfeit of scent, pouring forth
from thousands of open flower cups;
we long for fainter fragrance,
fewer flowers.

When the light strikes the chlorophyll
molecules, the electrons rise to higher
energy levels—said there,
to be in excited states.
We witness remarkable instances
of floral telepathy.

She sings in the capillary choir;
she is ravished by the garden,
tender petals,
red and blood-gorged paradise.
Tree branches cut and set as fence posts
take root and quickly branch.

Enter the perilous labyrinth,
                              like clay—
the key in Bk. XIII of the *Aeneid*.
And thus one is happy, measuring his garden by Virgil.
Rousseau sold his watch, began a new life.
Denis Diderot informed his father
he would follow no career at all;
he had no ambition.
Never more verve
and inspiration than after an orgy:
he would sit up all night writing.

And salt (it says) is extraordinarily
unambitious—like Diderot—
but clay? Clay has plans.
The memory of clay is manifest
in its ability to hold a pattern,
to influence its environment.
In the fifth stage of computer art
(clay art), the artist will be unnecessary,
in the way,
but he will be able to pull the plug.
In the sixth stage, pure disembodied energy
will have no plug, no plug,
no plug to pull.

This is a garden:

Pennyroyal quickens the brain
by smelling oft. Basil clears the wits.
Balm is for sympathy.

Bay for glory.
Ointments, liniments, plasters, cataplasms,
also saculi, little bags of flower petals,
pomanders, remarkable instances
of floral telepathy—
                    a mental stimulant,
red is warm and irritating. It aggravates
inflammatory conditions and increases
the activity of the male sex gland.
Amethyst light has the stimulating effects of red
and the tonic effects of blue.
Violet increases the activity of the female
sex gland. Then sit up all night writing.
Enter the perilous labyrinth:
the deforestation of upland China, 3000 B.C.,
the overgrazing of the Mediterranean basin,
the creation of the dust bowl of the Great Plains.

I was going to a house some friends bought,
Dove Street: the iconic implications of that
invokes a thousand poems. An old house,
large gilt mirrors, marble fireplaces,
spaces to breathe in. Three spinsters
had had a bookstore on the ground floor—
pretty hep—left their house
to the Edna Millay Society.

The City might work after all.
After all. The scene is coming around now
(perhaps not to be mentioned again).
The Scene. Poems are about cities. Odysseus
goes to the City, country boy, lots of shuffle
and ah! shucks, meets up with his *compadres*
and wrecks the place, but this is the kicker:
when he gets back to Ithaka it's the sticks—
like the Missouri towns I grew up in—and he says,
Good Lord, Penelope, we got to do
something about this place,
get a juke box and a pool hall.

—Music playing throughout the poem
and the clack of pool balls. The fact is,
If lions had language whomans wouldn't understand'em
　—
Ludwig Wittgenstein said that. Whoman's don't
understand much apart from the City,
and if there be dog shit on the sidewalk,
you don't try to talk to the dog.

Music throughout the poem, wind—the streets
of the City, like a maze in a garden, but not,
not for amusement, amazement. Half shame,
the city's history, built on trade,
skins, timber, and government, not legitimate
　　production.
H. James wrote fine sentences
on the hides of beavers, an animal,
to my memory, not mentioned in his thirty volumes.

Dog shit is like beavers, like sea shells
you bring back from the beach: they stand
for the speechless landscape,
which eludes the mighty glyph of the skyline.

I stopped an old man, talking to an unseen companion.
Who are you talking to?
　　　　　　　　　　Me brother thirty years dead.

You think we can talk with the dead?

Yes, but they don't talk back.

THE BOOK OF THE DEAD

*Always get rid of the private object in this way: assume that
it constantly changes, but that you do not notice the change
because your memory constantly deceives you.*

Forgetting the beginning of the sentence before
the beginning of the sentence lasts
to speak of war and country music
a) bomb, b) cancer, following
word by word with fingers prose
and the oranges of metaphysics
repealed and sectioned sweet.

Thus, said Henry Adams, the religious phase of civilization lasted 90,000 years; the mechanical has lasted for about 300. If the acceleration of history is following a progression, then, the electrical phase has a mind-expectancy of the square-root of 300, beginning about 1900. In 1917, we will enter a new age, lasting the square-root of 17.5 years; then one lasting the square-root of 4.18 year; then the square-root of 2.1 years. At some point, mind, no longer able to test any idea against the background of the age's general conception, disappeared.

I will stop in time drt drt
there in that river of slime and drt drt time
there in American earth's drt drt
imagined end, round and shining. I'll
make a pact drt drt
to fill the holes in
where the non-sense is
drt drt
the Land of the Dead
drt drt drt drt
The Land of the Dead the Land
of the Dead, wearing down the words, the wind
wears down the pyramids the pharoahs
drt drt:

we'll work in the dark—design
without knowledge, build
before research, go into production

without pilot plants—the Man-
hattan project Kekekekkow.
The Germans can build the A-bomb;
Al Einstein sez so, and Al
Einstein knows. Enrico
you lay the cornerstone.
He laid the cornerstone, graphite
brick. The pile grew, graphite brick—
Enrico, the joker. And the children?
Strontium 90 in their bones.
Iodine 131 drt drt in their thyroid glands

Kekekekkow

KekekekekekeKEoooOW.

CALL FOR A GENERAL STRIKE

1. Government has failed. No power is invested in the PUB-
LIC trust. All politics, therefore, is terrorism—the actions of indi-
viduals on behalf of private interests, in the name of the people, who
are said to hold title to the public reservoir of power. This is a
world-wide phenomenon.

2. In the middle of the seventeenth century, human beings began
to replicate themselves at an unprecedented rate. We may be run-
ning out of time and space. The world we have engineered—in
order to accommodate the numbers—is a vast artifice, our truest
work of art, and we inhabit it completely. It has no OUTSIDE.

The spectacular possibility of atomic war persists, of course, but
now life on the planet is threatened by inert gasses we spray into the
atmosphere from aerosol cans of deodorant, by the possibility of
man-made micro-organisms to which we have no immunity, the
inglorious destruction of fertile farm land and oxygen-making
forests.

The great catastrophe might bring an ultimate moment of tragic self-awareness. We might see by the light of the fire-storms in the moments following a nuclear war spasm what we have not been able to otherwise see. But it is at least as likely that meaningless and hopeless complexities will multiply until the simplest acts will become overwhelming, and even the most vital will lose their taste for living.

3. Superstition and idolatry have never been so common, especially among the educated classes. We are so captivated by our ignorance that we call it knowledge. Education is initiation into the rites (rights) of private power. The motive of knowledge is greed.

Consider—as a critique of the current state of knowledge—a cultural enterprise which would establish power for PUBLIC use equivalent to the power which knowledge of the law of conservation of matter and energy delivered into private hands. There is a kind of knowledge which is useful only when it is shared, like locks which are opened by two keys, held by two people. The knowledge of language as such is of this nature. Of course, for the most part, language is used as earth is, for private purposes: it is used to say what this or that person thinks or feels, to give orders, to make contracts between private parties, to objectify the anguish of our isolation.

4. Poetry cannot solve these problems, but nothing LESS than poetry can solve them. This is difficult to speak of: perhaps I can think of all art as being something like architecture. Is it possible to create forms which are not expressions of the architect, the Board of Directors, of the Great Man or the faceless bureaucracy—forms which are SPECIFIC to everyone involved in their use? The purest formalism demonstrates the possibility of such art, but then architecture is never purely formal: its content is not steel and concrete but lives.

The failure of functionalism was not theoretical. Rather the functions which its forms sought to follow were dreary and tedious. An office building, where the primary functions are typing and filing, is certain to give rise to a form which is itself an image of ennui and habitual activity required of vested private power.

5. But, first, you must be a poet, someone said, demonstrating elegantly the rhetoric which leaves the discussion suspended.

WRONG.
First, you must stop.
STOP
     STOP
     STOP   STOP   STOP
I am preparing to utter a most general word
        EVERYTHING
      Stop everything.

6. Things make sense because they go on. I am demonstrating this truth. After some time I will stop. Our diaphragms will go into uncontrollable spasms. It will be a painful experience for some, and we will all be frightened. This will be laughter. Some will fall, rolling and pounding on the earth or floor. We must expect some casualties. Some will be made unhappy by their laughter. We will need to treat them gently. During the following months, the fits of laughter will recur, when politicians, priests, and others who seek to return us to our senses rise to speak. There will be silence and laughter. In time we will learn to trust the moral significance of this sign. Then someone will begin to speak.

    And someone began to speak,
or the Land of the Dead began to speak,
ugly mouths of caves, work, and so forth, forth.
On Beethoven's desk was a pendulum clock
in the form of a pyramid,
where was engraved the alabaster head of a woman;
Tom T. Hall's swimming pool has the shape of a guitar.

Text is cancer.
The text is cancer.
The Book of Going Forth by Day is cancer.

The Book of Going Forth into Night is cancer.
The most intractable, variable
and incomprehensible form of cellular derangement.
A kidney cell stays in the kidney,
a lung cell in the lung.
Cancer cells belong nowhere.
They have no homes, like Americans,
like boll weevil, like money,
like Americans, like truck drivers,
night-shift operators and insomniacs:

      WWNC, Asheville
      WHAS, Louisville
      WSM, Nashville
      XENT, Laredo, Texas.

Patent medicines, evangelists, and chick farms,
country music,
               colluvies of wild opinionists,
swarmed into the remote wilderness. Honey,
I got the time:
following the calculations of the *Zohar*,
they fix't 1648 as the *annus mirabilis*;
following the book of *Daniel*, William Miller
fix't 1843; Halley's comet's next
scheduled appearance is 1986.
What are the pyramids anyway?
The equivalent of our space rockets—
devices for securing anyway
at extravagant cost
passage to heaven for the favored few.
The Pharoah's desires were too
easily satisfied—
time hung heavy,
so ladened with days he was stone
and Egyptian technology mostly song
and dance.

I'd won a prize in the Arthur Godfrey
Talent Search, playing a dobro
and singing original songs, but of course
this is New York in the 1950's
with memories of the Great War.
Who a century hence will believe
it was not an elaborate hoax,
complete with tons of documentation
in the Library of Congress—an effort as exhausting
as building the pyramids? Future Scholars
will demonstrate the entire nation was employed—
even prosperously so—and J.
Edgar Hoover, who loved his mom
and dog, directed this longest movie
and the sequels continued to appear
almost to the beginning of the third millennium.
Slide trombones you couldn't count—they stepped
so smartly—and the music almost unbearable.
They called Central Park John Lennon Field.
Expensive tenants on Park Avenue
said the air was better. Beat, beat.
They called acid rain sweet water
(Thus Poetry and Ecological Technology:
A Second Look).

History is not an organ(ism)
                              breathe
or if it is an organ
                    breathe now

we can like Bach improvise on it
                                   breathe now
                                   breathe
                                   breathe.

Time keeps thumping—still
it isn't going anywhere
                    beat
                        beat

the bears are asleep
heart
beat.
Mankind can bear breathe a helluvareality.
It must
     beat   beat   it bears it all.
Thinking doesn't change matters that much.
And it bears the reality of unreality—
its wooden flutes of revery,
and side two in just a moment—
animals in the radio—creaking doors—
becoming animals—and a certain nervousness—
texture, flow
in more than one direction,
to promise an end that never comes.
History cannot end as history;
for it to end, beat
as history
it must exceed itself,
drt drt.

If you want to play
music, you have to play more than notes
you have to play music—

      Charlie Christian died young
      Fats Navarro died young
      Charlie Parker died young
      Clifford Brown died young
      Booker Ervin died young
      Eric Dolphy died young
      John Coltrane died young
      Bud Powell went crazy
       no one remembers Milt Buckner
and country music went slick.

O America you skin your musicians alive,
and what became of the Monk,
the Monk, the Monk?

                        The text is Cancer.
Text is cancer.
Did you hear about the fire
in Mommsen's house, destroyed all his notes,
history gone up in flame?
And Dr. Baker moved to Laredo,
opened a radio station across the border—
power levels not allowed by the FCC.
One citizen began to hear XENT
in his mouth: one of his teeth
was a small crystal set and transducer.
Did you hear? at Oak Ridge:
the most powerful magnet ever built:
hammers and screwdrivers jerked
from workers' hands; hairpins
flew suddenly into the air.
Then the reactor became critical again,
like a dead monster coming to life
and starting to breathe. Turtles
were newcomers on the Triassic scene—
extraordinary animals, so successful they are
more or less unchanged the last 200 million years.

      WWVA, Wheeling
      WSM, Nashville
      KWTO, Springfield
      WBAP, Forth Worth—

Drink, divorce, infidelity, and tragedy,
Black Drought and Wine of Cardui,
unrequited love and tragedy,
dance music and gospel music,
crying steel guitars and ladybug mandolins,
a Roman Empire of declines and falls—
hands like lizards, green lizards,
with blue heads;
                    the seven planes of the human face—
the greater and lesser planes,
                        the size of the eyes:

the skin, then outer-space,
turtles unchanged for 200 million years.
Man may be a flash in the pan—
the *pika*, the Japanese say, the flash.
Dear Dr. Baker:
My nose, left cheek, and ear
                                           were rotting away
with cancer. I had been to great doctors,
from Chi
            cago to Denver,
but after using your liniment only three weeks
I was healed.

Millions of years passed,
primitive jawless fishes appeared,
plants wandered onto the land
and various animals without backbones.
Then reptiles appeared and grew larger,
grew larger and extinct—the dire lizards;
the world thenceforth dominated by mammals
for some time dominated by and by.
Neanderthal man dominated,
had laryngeal equipment to produce
grunts and snorts. He dominated
mammals, with clubs or bare hands,
and he did not speak, but he danced
and he died (sorta) unht
hrrn ghtn—history cancers, work.

Weisskopf worked by feel (Los Alamos):
What is the plutonium
cross-section at 2.5 million volts?
He would go into a trance
ghnt hrrnt—names of gods
without full-voiced vowels—and say 2.2.
Von Neumann watched Weisskopf,
designed computers. Hank Williams said,
When a hillbilly sings a crazy song,
he feels crazy. When he sings,

I Laid My Mother
Away,
          he sees her a-layin
right there in the coffin.
You got to know a lot about hard work.
You got to have smelt a lot
of mule manure
before you can sing like a hillbilly.
And the period of Egyptian
unification coincides with mass graves,
where many cracked skulls are found.

The mace, not the bronze age chariot,
established the One King, the force
which was a magnet (at Oak Ridge).
His hair was blue.
The Pharoah's mace hung heavy.
He was bored. He cracked skulls, spoke vowels,
and other complexities. The primal need
for order and achievement by
increasingly formal repetitive acts—
fro and to—the guilt, a smell,
or vision accompanies each repetition,
imperfect, imperfections take shape
and grow. A-laying
right there in the coffin.
The text is cancer,
and the architecture of feedback deletion
unclear. The difference between normal cells
and cancer cells must lie in the chemistry
of deoxyribonucleic acids,
which fail to inscribe the proper synthesis
of enzymes, of tissues and proteins,
thereby permitting metastasis and invasion.
It kicks over the traces of genetics,
and, free of mama, papa, church, given
paradigmatic gestures, revealing the original
ontology and the somatic template
which strikes it out

and sets it on the circuitous paths to death:
an offensive based on fast carrier
task forces and hard-hitting amphibious groups,
as stepping stones across the ocean.
The plants were early explorers of the land,
and soon after they were accompanied
by animals, without backbones,
ancestors of insects: fossils
show this transition.
                              Vertebrates
have crossed a threshold, and cancer
is one of the prices they've had to pay—
letting feedback go, planning factories
before the product has been invented:
acres of plumbing at Oak Ridge,
functioning with precision
never conceived in engineering history,
Weisskopf's trances, von Neumann's machines.
The number of chromosome rearrangements
in each generation of multiplying tumor cells
represents a clear manifestation, observed
under the microscope.
                              I didn't know
God made honky-tonk angels.
                              How could I?
May be degenerate cells
or fragment of cells, having somehow—
wild-cat woman
                 and tom-cat man—
rid themselves of all unnecessary features,
except their hereditary apparatus
in the form of nucleic acids
and their protective and infective apparatus
in the form of protein—
self destructive processes of life,
taking on living formalism,
suicidal chreods of cellular metabolism.
And to be of such intelligence (Akhnaton's)
in the eighteenth dynasty was to court disaster.

Had he not been a visionary
(O! had some polytheistic compromise applied),
but the pyramid is empty,
                              as well as empty.
And DNA from an infectious virus
(phage X174) was introduced into the test tube
as a printing press for its duplication;
to it were added nucleotides of adenine,
thymine, quanine, cytosine, and DNA replicase.
Not only did the viral DNA copy itself,
but it was biologically active,
for it was infectious.

MacArthur stood on the bridge of the *Nashville*,
corncob pipe in his teeth
(strains of *Turkey in the Straw* in the background).

Leyte's irregular shape has been compared to
a molar tooth,
a rough-hewn winged Victory of Samothrace
(slightly damaged)
and a misshapen hour-glass,
a small dog running from left to right,
forelegs amputated at the thighs,
hind legs outstretched, ears and tail flying,
mouth open.
Now stand this dog on his heels,
so his head point north.
Extending north from Ormoc to Corigora Bay,
the Ormoc valley is the collar,
and to the east, a heavily forested
central mountain range
runs from the dog's shoulder to the hind quarters and tail.

And why should the phytosaurs have become extinct?
Excellently adapted to the predatory life,
to the end of their days no reptile
could challenge them, but they disappeared.

The crocodilians grew larger,
imitated the phytosaurs in uncanny fashion.

Why did the phytosaurs leave their strategy
to the crocodiles?

The underwater swimmers reported a line
of well-camouflaged pillboxes, trenches
and dug-outs along the southern beaches.
Less of the tumor genome is being transcribed
into the messenger RNA of those regions
(the skin of the dog)
of the genome undergoing transcription. Dr. Baker,
my nose, left cheek, and ear were rotting away,
and the addition of history
to DNA markedly reduces its ability
to act as a template for the synthesis.
Roy Acuff sang, Cowards over Pearl Harbor,
and he sang, The Great Speckled Bird—
fiddle, five-string banjo, and rhythm guitar,
string bass and dobro.

Within a few minutes of H-hour,
soldiers of four divisions were running,
creeping, or crawling across the sandy beaches
of Leyte.
               They knocked out half-a-dozen pill-boxes
and pressed forward, through foul-smelling
water and slime, often up to their waists (wastes,
scared, wouldn't you be? the way
the enemy can see in the dark,
and you'd never eat your carrots).
You didn't know how to die (you hadn't
seen the movies), so when the machine gunners
were hit, you shifted, you and your comrades,
to their places, and when you were hit,
you did not know how to die because
you had not seen the movies, and when

you were hit, your comrades tried to drag you
to the rear, but you were hit, and you died,
not knowing how, proving
education isn't everything,
as the defenders crawled on their bellies
and slithered through mud and long grass.
Your comrades hurled grenades through firing
apertures or stuffed them down ventilation shafts.
The Japanese (these Japanese) were killed
in a few minutes.
The horses died more slowly.
And it rained. It rained night and day.
It rained and blew.

Some diluvialists let imagination run riot:
might the resultant cooling effect snowball
into an ice age?
Ice flowing down hill,
sluggishly, picking up material in its Ptah,
chunks of bed-rock, stones, and boulders
frozen into glaciers;
the glaciers, the teeth
of a file, smoothing, polishing, sometimes
scratching,
                    the rock pavement over which the ice moveth.
And were there glaciers still in the Baltic
when civilization dawned bright and clear in Egypt?

Hank Snow sang, I'm Moving On:
                              who'd have thought
the conventional manner of using a shovel
would repay the scientific study of expert
investigators?
                    178,000 bucks the first year.
The actuating equipment fits into the shoveler's
pocket,
          and the two wires leading to the pea bulbs
for either hand are unnoticeable,

when fed through the sleeves of the operator's
overalls.

        The bulbs are fixed by adhesives
to the hands.

Given sufficient power,
the operator might travel between two points
without traversing the intervening distances.
Given the idea of non-space by-pass, where
do we stand? O! where
do we stand. How in the enlargements
of the fifth dimension, how
are we guided to our (fateful) destination?
And how do we regain the conventional universe,
when the wheelbarrow is full.
This is a navigational problem of the first order.
And is this the reason the phytosaurs became extinct?

Millions of years pass.
The first primitive jawless fishes appear,
the plants give up the pleasure dome of the sea,
accompanied by spineless animals,
forebearers of mosquitoes, horseflies, cockroaches,
the successful frogs and dire lizards—
the luckless beasts come
and come and go
and go.

And then the flash:
as in homo erectus,
it has the bun-shaped protrusion of the occiput,
the boney brow ridge, the relatively flattened crown,
that from the rear resembles a gambrel roof.
Traces of cancer in Java man, the mummies
from the pyramids of Gizeh.
Not satisfied
with uncontrolled growth, the cancer cells
penetrate blood streams,

                                lymph stream
which become poisoned underground rivers.

And in the force field the skin of space
puckers, before passing through the induced rent,
which heals behind the soul,
going forth into non-space—
the hypothesis of cosmic censorship,
the viral theory of writing. Egypt
enjoyed a near monopoly on writing paper
and the making of glass eyes (intended
originally for mummies). The literature of Greece
was written on papyrus of the Nile.

Instruct us, please,
tell us how the world will end:

it begins as the drama of an execution sale;
if you look at it long enough
it becomes a democracy, with a constitution
(intended for mummies).
The cosmos is almost entirely light,
but photons have no opinions—a defect
we correct, having opinions on their behalf;
we have chiliastic light

                        on behalf of glass eyes.

I am the great egg in Kenkenur
(the Great Cackler).
I live; it liveth.
I become old, I live—
mostly light;
I snuff the air;
I see a tree;
I see a tree;
deal me a hand;
I don't want

the whole deck
anymore; I have
opinions,
a pocket watch,
a necktie with palm trees;
I see my hand,
my writer's knot,
a crescent scar
on my right thumb;
I will hear nothing,
not even silence
fluttering its aching wings.

Then grave worry descended
over Manhattan Project Headquarters
in the Woolworth Building:
they didn't have adequate diffusion screens
or adequate pumps for Oak Ridge.
And Hank Williams was fired
from the Grand Ole Opry—drunkenness, chronic
instability. Dr. Brinkley plugged
his goat-gland operation, from XERA,
Villa Acuña. Dear Dr. Brinkley,
I couldn't, and Slim Whitman
sang *Indian Love Call.*
John Wilkinson introduced drills for boring cannons.
Bored cannons used standardized balls,
standardized balls. Dear Dr. Brinkley,
I hadn't for years. The cannon was bored.
Now at 73 I have married
and started a new family.
It takes a heap of voices to sing a millennial song.
I have opinions, a pocket watch.
I'm almost an A-bomb—
born about the same year.

You can say the stereospondyl became extinct,
because it reached the end of its rope.
From stem pseudosuchians evolved larger

pseudosuchians, including heavy
armored quadrupeds,
and they reached the end of their ropes.
Private Harold H. Moon was isolated.
During four hours of constant combat, he
threw grenades, fired his machine gun and the weapons
of his fallen comrades.
He directed mortar fire,
yelled curses and challenges,
dueled with a Japanese officer for a solid hour
and finally shot him in the head.
An entire platoon charged his foxhole,
yelling, To hell with Roosevelt,
to hell with Babe Ruth,
to hell with Roy Acuff,
and he reached the end of his rope.

Enrico Fermi made bets with his colleagues:
would the bomb ignite the atmosphere?
And if it did, would it destroy only New Mexico
or the entire world? Work for me,
Kenkenur, you Great Cackler,
that the architecture of feedback deletion be known,
and the memory of evil things leave my mouth.
The Japanese carrier, the Maya, was hit four times
and sank into the pleasure dome of the sea.
The presence of mineral, animal, and plant life
(plankton) contributes to the green appearance
of water; brown, red, and yellow can be due
to brown algae and swarms of copepods;
patches of olive green, to swarms of diatoms.
We are familiar with red water from rusty pipes,
green water in stagnant pools,
and possibly yellow water from sulphur springs,
but there is also luminous water.
Luminous water!
LUMINOUS WATER!

The whole country was lighted by a searing light the intensity many times that of the midday sun. It was golden, purple, violet, gray, and blue. It lighted every peak, crevasse and ridge of the nearby mountain range with a clarity and beauty that cannot be described but must be seen to be imagined. It was that beauty poets dream about but describe most poorly and inadequately. Thirty seconds after the explosion came, first the air blast pressing hard against people and things, to be followed almost immediately by the strong, sustained awesome roar which warned of doomsday and made us feel that we puny things were blasphemous to dare tamper with forces heretofore reserved for the almighty.

—Thus, Brig. Gen. Farrell,
to the Secretary of War.

The Japanese soldier,
clad in sabre and loin cloth,
studied his dictionary and said,
Me vanquished miserable dishonored depraved.

The Germans had made no effort to build the bomb.

THE DEAD DON'T HAVE BOOKS

Forget, forget, *that you are having these experiences yourself.*

Faye is dead now, the oldest.
Pac, Bill, Homer, and Paul are dead:
each third spring

        death requires one of the family.

Don't follow that thought—
I know there is magic;

        I don't have to practice it.

And Paul said, Don't look back.

I inhabit the don't look back of I-go.
People who give clear directions are servants of God.

I can show you a place in northeastern Arizona red mesa country, and in a space of ten miles you can take in by a single view, the red fades to pink and light grey. You begin to climb into scrub, piñon, birch, aspen, and on up into virgin stands of ponderosa pine.

It doesn't mean a thing until I tell you about it. Then we are standing on the north rim of the Grand Canyon. The Land of Death is beautiful; a hot wind blows from it. I believe it's mistaken, somehow, that there should be such a place: one-hundred million man-made deaths this century, mostly *man*-made. Man-woman unmade.

The death machine is a factual object, a philosophic object, uncertain of definition, yet a mechanism so intuitively whole that the 'I' itself becomes subject to analysis as its component.

The don't look back of I-go—
the microdot technique, photo
reduction of secret information disguised
as a period or the dot of an ego.
You can change your mind.
If you smear your body
with human fat you are irresistable.

You can change your entire mind.
Eclipses are normal—
caused by a heavenly body obstructing
the light of another.
They are not caused by the evils
of politicians.
You have time to change your mind.
He threw the Bible to the floor
and kicked it back and forth,
whilst proclaiming:

    White people have tails
    White people have tails
    White people have tails.

You can change your mind,
without reserve.
Thus history, triggers, millennial events.
No gesture so hopeless
as a change of mind?
Earth also is a shock wave,
a cliff also sun's rays
fall down.

Now life is an underground erosion of the cliff;
the energy stored as noble chemicals
begins its slow decline,
its sometimes slow decline—
are you having fun?

No motion proceeds in one direction forever
(it says)
       with the exception of evolutionary processes?
it asks (parenthetically),
so everything but everything is
rhythm?
     So the beat isss
always dragging its feet across the strand,

tracks from proteinoids to arboreal mammals,
from arboreal mammals to two-legged
upright, walking predators, and on
(the soul became a violin in Cremona—
it had long been a woman)
to Beethoven, listening
to Cherubini's *Medea* on a music box
and a music box,
listening to Beethoven's string quartets
in the XXIst century.
In the XXIst century the eyes of the people are small,
their ears are radar screens, mecanthropoids,
scanning the air for traces of music,
the music is small.

A nostalgia for dissonance
sustains small bands in the mountains, guerillas,
guitar pickers, nomads on mules:
the thing they love become the thing
they fear.
                    the music mis-remembered,
the thing they fear become
the thing they desire.
It takes a lot of voices to sing a millennial song.
A rising of peasants calling themselves
Bagadae (Celtic: vagabonds),
the circumcellionists of North Africa,
and the Whitmanian singers of the open road:
the Okies started down near Brawley,
worked their way up the coast to Santa Barbara,
then over to the central valley,
and on north to Washington state.
We're always hearing of the death of poetry,
the death of the theater,
the death of the printed word.
The cells have entered the valley
and the river, not far from the source,
is below. Hugh said, You're likely to make it
(the XXIst century).

For me it's touch and go.
These indigestible materials pile up in the lysosomes,
which swell to enormous proportions,
overloading the lysosomes,
causing lethal cellular damage.
Before accepting the theory of an outside invasion,
consider Tay-Sachs, Niemann-Pick, Hurley, Hunter,
Fabray, Goucher, and Pompé diseases.
These hopeless events pile up in the psychosomes,
which swell to enormous proportions,
overloading the psychosomes,
so the music fades:
consider Beethoven's deafness,
resulting from faulty plotting in the family romance.
His father was a wastrel,
second-rate musician, toady,
probable informer and police agent,
inadequate provider and hapless extortionist.
The family romance permits imaginary seizures,
seizures, seizures
of parental authority: thus Beethoven's
royal parentage,
and the resultant damage to the psychosomes
(thus most *apologiae poeticae*).

Whatever is in the king's box,
it could be empty,
as well as empty.
Whoever is on the king's couch,
it is empty:
for the king, by his leave, cannot coin English
as he could coin money
(cannot coin German or Beethoven).
Consider the psychobiology of sadness:
Mausolus is remembered for his tomb—
such pathetic immobility.
A world without things is impossible,
unimaginable, impossible.
We cannot love a shadow.

His queen drank his ashes in wine
and pined away.
They are both in the British Museum.
Whatever is in the Mausoleum of Halicarnassus,
it is empty, empty, empty.
In the year 1000 the heir to the German throne
was six years old.
In France a youth of twenty
held the royal crown.
In Italy, no royal power,
no Emperor of the West:
Guy and Lambert of Spoleto were dead;
Berengar failed to resist
the Hungarian invaders (thus, lost support
of people, great and little).
Arnulf was seized by numbness
in the head. Marizoa died
and prudently Hugh married Bertha,
Rudolf's widow. Otto's army
pursued the Hungarians to Regensburg,
where Conrad the Red fell,
pierced in the throat by an arrow.

Grievous irregularities in celebrating Holy Mass,
simony and sacrilege, adultery and lust so constant
the sacred palace of the popes was a brothel,
violence, murder, arson, playing with dice
and praying to Jupiter and Venus for aid,
fictitious speeches, fabulous numbers,
startling qualities of mind, and unusual physical details.
The logothete insulted Otto by speaking of him
not as emperor but merely as King.

Beyond the city stretched the dark and solitary salt
    marshes,
dotted here and there with huts of solitaries,
dedicated to prayer.
Otto spent the spring of 1001 (the space odyssey)

in wandering supplication to heaven for the future
and in penance for the past.

This is a process resembling death,
a proteinoid without nucleic acids has no
informational guidance. Error, therefore,
predominates and leads to short-lived proteinoids,
incapable of going beyond initial formation.
Without sigma the polymerase begins to transcribe
at any point along the molecule
and without rho it does not terminate
the molecular sentence,
                              a process resembling death, a
and leads to short-lived proteinoids incapable of
the polymerase begins to transcribe at any
without rho it does not terminate the molecular sentence
    this is
no informational
and leads to short-lived proteinoids incapable of
to transcribe at any point along the molecule this is
it does not terminate the
is death, a process resembling death,
a proteinoid without nucleic acids
guidance. Error, therefore, predominates and leads
going beyond initial formation,
without sigma the polymerase begins to
any point along the molecule and without rho
molecular sentence and those
in this universe of hard numbers, they knew that a
night at the bank and
home late if a halfpenny were
resembling death, a proteinoid
and leads to short-lived proteinoids, incapable of going
    beyond
polymerase begins to transcribe at
terminate the molecular sentence and those
universe of hard numbers. They knew that a balance
and that everyone would be home late if
those who invented purposes for living grew up

knew that a balance had to be struck each night at
home late if a halfpenny were missing
purposes for living grew up in
to be struck each night
home late if a halfpenny
and those who invented purposes for living
grew up in this universe of hard numbers.
They knew that a balance had to be struck
each night at the bank
and that everyone would be home late
if a halfpenny were missing.
For this reason the universe of hard numbers
is colorless, and I attended a bacchanal
(in the universe of hard numbers),
where I had to laugh a great deal,
with the result that today
I have had to cry as heartily.

We are transistors, in the literal sense:
power-minded, cosmos-centered, semi-conductors.
Common sense was what kingship lacked,
almost by definition.

I was on Broadway, with Zubin Mehta,
almost by definition,
and the orchestra was improvising—
flowers, tulips,
as you'd expect of a Dutch city like New York,
and crocuses as in any city,
where spring comes late and a little
color is a hopeful sign,
but also tropical flowers,
birds of paradise and orchids,
which poets write of etymologically,
and other plants of southern and persistently
steamy terrains, palms
and bromeliads so primitive
I expected to see dire lizards.
By this time my seersucker suit

was beginning to be hotter than I liked,
and the Maestro, who is a cool character,
was sweating too. He said,
Let's go into the Penny Arcade.
It's air conditioned. We can have
a soft drink and a cigarette.
But before we were well settled
into our video football, a youth
lost at *Space Invaders* and the solar
system was being destroyed: Uranus,
Saturn, Jupiter. I was afraid
it would end like this, the Maestro said. Quick,
get under the pin-ball machine.
Or can the poet speak
to the royal Mechanthropoid.

I said, I'll try

ON PHYSIS [i.e. nature], OR THE NON-EXISTENT

Was the topic I announced, hoping
to warm to the classical subject
and demonstrate that the non-existent
could not be
destroyed—a Gestapo of nouns,
a Buchenwald of verb tenses,
the syntax of Hiroshima and Nagasaki.
The Soul in Cremona became a violin,
stained with varnish of a lost formula.
Even the therapist who treats depressed
patients with tricyclics and monamine oxidase
must inquire about the dynamics of the anguish,
the plastic nature of the mantle, the fractured
state of the crust accounting for vulcanism.
Language ceases to be useful for communication
and becomes, rather, a source of distortion
of time and space, power and order,
recurrent movements of moon and sun,

flood and storm and earthquake,
divine mechantropoidship and public works,
which will have begun about the time
the Roman Emperors were portrayed
realistically and the river cuts
westward in search of another agreement,
regarding Day-light Savings Time
and the balance of your check book.

The polluting material does not disappear,
so where does the Self go?
and if its whereabouts are not evident,
are we entitled to ask, What is it
polluting now?
Agreement is incomplete,
which behaviors are indicative of fear—
nose picking and hand fumbling may be fear related.
Digit sucking was not monitored in this study.
Children rapidly approached and played with
the new toys. With toy prams and telephones
latency to manipulate was virtually zero—
the literature on stranger-fear, the validation
of the wariness construct.
What constitutes-wariness?

What constitutes a musical idea?
The former question is simpler
(but not so intriguing).
As the team runs down the field,
the computer, intriguing at the speed of light,
constructs a model of the strategy and makes
predictions about where the goal will be crossed
(with ever increasing reliability, at the speed of light)
and directs, by radio, a ruthless linebacker
to the point.

The more perfect the defense becomes,
the more offense depends upon the arbitrary

will of the ball carrier. Distance, thus,
becomes a function of the will and the intriguing
terrain: the *li* is a measure of distance in China,
like the mile (our mile, it says). The *li*
is shorter where the going is easy, down hill,
on the Interstate, longer against a tough defense.
Consider the psychobiology of distances
and the sadness involved.
Our sadness?
A knowledge of the soul of things
is a new and direct way of discovering
the soul of man (and his sadness)?
The soul became a violin in Cremona:
the object of longing replaced by expression of longing
and its sadness.
In *The Book of the Dead*
pronouns are interrogatory
or impersonal.

Men have murdered for salt.   Wars
have been fought over salt mines.   It has
been used for food and embalming.
The soul of salt is violent;
it is also a preservative.
Sugar is a conflict product.
Some foods are bisexual—roast chicken and oranges.
People do not feel so good about taking vitamin
pills as they do about drinking buttermilk.
Crackers are lazy bread; prunes
are contrary to nature. There are powerful
words in the vocabulary of constipation—purge,
catharsis, elimination,
irregularity.

　　Pierre Jacquet's automaton
holds a quill pen in his right hand,
his head and eyes in subtle motion,
constant, intent,
weighted with his sole self

and more, the urban crisis of himself.
How long is slow
death?

In his cups they all passed,
confusedly before him,
the hermaphrodites whisper
to the rose-breathers the secrets of impossible love,
the Bagadae bear to him women
with magical green and yellow eyes,
the mechanthropoids dance with elastic feet,
and he hears the shrill cry of the Circumcellionists.
The column of Panchaia unveils its mysteries:
he is in business (the book a ledger);
he is the history of Europe and America,
leading to the Second Great War.
Pages back he had written, *This is a River*,
now he is coming to the mouth. He dips
his quill in ink, shakes it twice,
and commences to write:

California is described as a large
country in the West Indies.
It invented the movies.
It is reached by following a star,
your favorite star.
You are allowed the choice:

Because I see her eye
open
begonias growing therein
because this love comes walking one foot
and then the other from the East
this is a terminus.

Because her light casts deep
shadows in my eyes
the begonia smiles

because my hands are air
or like air or trouble
or without callouses they are
gloved begrimed shy because
the techniques of explanation are like
violin music in moonlight
because of her menstrual cycle
this is a terminus.

Because she has no body
I wrestle a shadow
in this irregular polyhedron
hip against her idea
because listening to Mozart
makes me dangerously rational
I think
because otherwise
the sky would be silent
because I would hear the sky
again I am listening to the sky
because this is a terminus
this is a terminus.

What constitutes a risible idea?
What constitutes the risible
construct of history?
How many singers does it take
to sing a millennial song?
How can slow drt drt
death drt drt
take so long drt
drtdrt drt   drt

The WPA excavated a brontosaurus,
northwestern Cimmaron County,
Elzy Tanner's farm, and petrified logs,
redwood-like trees, six feet in diameter.
Inland seas have ebbed and flowed

across the Dust Bowl. Too much
wind, dirt, flatness, space,
barbed-wire, uncertainty.

In 1495 an English peasant could earn
enough in fifteen weeks to provision
his household for a year;
by 1610 he could not well provision
his household by working constantly,
by working constantly and further from home.
Towns were electrical transformers,
increasing tensions, accelerating rhythms.
We are transistors.

    Positive
feedback
leads
to accelerated
motion
and breakdown
manic states
psychosomatic
illnesses.

Chloroplasts and mitochondria
were invaders, taking up residence
in other cells, and a class Dionysiac merchants arose.
Redundancy is applied to overcome noise
and refutation. Music
in competition with other sounds?
Who would refute a phrase of Beethoven?
The theme of principles and variations:
the OED in a magnetic memory core,
Shönberg's book on harmony in the memory core.
Nietzsche suffered
118 days of migraines that year.
The physiological possibilities of organic life
exhausted some two million years ago

and few improvements since—
say a few
in the complexity of primate nervous systems.
I'm posing here a question of political economy
the pri´vate´ nervous system.
How many millionaires planned their mausoleums:
the vogue of the Rubáiyát
came precisely
during the decade of unashamed wealth,
and it's a far cry
from molecules in solution to organized cells.
Can we think of a coding system
(O! can we think?)
of a coding system before
the product of the code is known?
How did this cozy relationship
between nucleic acids and proteinoids begin?

Exchanges of material must occur
across the outer boundary of the cell.
Energy must be expended
to maintain the barrier
and to surmount it. Imperialism
is a relationship between a Center
and a Periphery nation (manic states)
so that:

  1) there is a harmony of interest between the center in the Center
and the center in the Periphery;
  2) there is more disharmony of interest within the Periphery than
within the Center;
  and 3) there is disharmony of interest between the periphery in
the Center and the periphery in the Periphery.

Better do that again: *return to 1 above.*

This may be the end of the poem.
We may never get beyond it,
though it is not a satisfying end—
a process resembling death. Plague
erupted in Kirgiz,
the primordial plague reservoir:
from the center of the Center the Black Death
spread to China and India and then West
to Turkistan. There were murmurings
about plague. People saw coffins in air and flames,
heard sounds of distant cannons.
Genoese traders were trapped in Koffa,
besieged by the Janiberg Kipchak Kahn.
The Kahn held siege for years,
before his long-limbed warriors began to die.
Furious he ordered the plague-infested corpses
catapulted over the walls of the city.

The great Genoese galleys winched up
their anchors, loosened sails from yardarms,
and bore off to the western seas. The mortality
lasted seven months.

It was of two-types:
the first lasted two months,
with continuous fever and spitting of blood,
and from this one died in three days;
the second lasted the rest of the period,
also with continuous fever
but with apostumes and carbuncles,
principally on the armpits and groins.
From this one died in five days.
He (Jacquet's automaton) designed the control loop
to obey the Law of Requisite Variety
and to meet the provisions of Shannon's tenth theorem:
control, therefore, is implicitly possible.
I said he was a kabalist, and he thought I said a catalyst,
implicitly, but I said, No,
that a machine cannot write music like Beethoven

is no refutation,
for what other human can?
And he said I was a kabalist,
and I thought he said a capitalist.
Good Lord! No! I cried. The deaths of Mozart
and his esteemed friend, Marianne van Genzinger,
had affected Haydn deeply. Furthermore,
he was conducting more or less simultaneous love affairs:
more with the London Widow, Rebecca Schröter,
less with the singer, Luigia Polzelli—
small wonder he was a poor teacher to Beethoven.
Such malfunctions may also occur in computers:
current flows through the closed loops,
loops of components,
causing schizophrenia,
through the closed loops.

Now the two-legged, upright, walking predator is relieved of being human. Machines can do that for him and bear the burden of intelligence and its peculiar diseases. The predator was never good at it anyway and turned to predation largely because pattern recognition and the required ritual taxed his capacities beyond the limits of control. He thought he might use his mind, rather than being used by it. The cruelty of this thought will be recognized in all of his political traditions. The epoch we have passed through, in which mind used the laughing biped against his will and partially without his knowledge for its own purposes, has ended with Babbage, von Neumann, and the nameless geniuses of IBM. The biped's generators of discontinuity, uniqueness, and difference, his ability to follow a track which follows no pattern, can be allowed unimpeded play. It is possible to laugh. This ability has been taken gravely and called mysticism. It is the ability to laugh.

    The brake lever is a brake lever
only when it is connected with a brake.

Also a throttle is,
and so forth:

processes resembling a language,
resembling a finale of chromatic music,
the universe of hard numbers,
musical snuff boxes,
digital living and elegant computers, fine
craftsmanship—
epiphenomena of a central control which does not exist.

The heart of the computer is the electronic
dictionary. Copy
(of what?)
is punched into the magnetic-core memory.
We're approaching the river of Forgetfulness. We're
leaving this electromagnetic memorial (of whom?),
this trace to fill out the lines
and supply hyphens where necessary.
Then the tape goes to the linecaster.
Television-like signals write characters
on moving webs of dye-coated paper.

Filoruxad
        Vybe,
he stuttered.
Abeh twad filoruxad.
Efiloruxad tux beh qux vybeh.
Fim noruxad filos vybe.

The alphabet cycle grinds to a halt;
the Mill of the Ages is stilled.
Limits of production accepted
and loved.
Loved
is the hard part.

THE BOOK OF THE FATHER

How could human behavior be described? surely only by sketching the actions of a variety of humans, as they are all mixed up together. What determines our judgment, our concepts and reactions, is not what one man is doing *now, an individual action, but the whole hurly-burly of human actions, the back-ground against which we see any action.*

Saeta. Sun light on iron railing where a cat walks making a shadow where a song had been.

Solea. I thought I was Hart Crane's last bear in the Ozarks. I was my body was I was heavy. Slung on my spine, better bear I was, so slung, heavy, chest, torso untiring eyes bear, eating fish, berries, setting example for the person I was, with gimpy tongue and tired brain. No time to think: fish, that quick. Don't think, my pupil, youth, with red hair and dull eyes, to hit the water *before* the fish arrives. Try it. No try it: he was a responsibility, a shadow when I sought my solitude in the thighs of a mate. He followed and his shadow in my rage for solitude of a mate I mistook for myself, the son, the last bear, etc.

Clinamen. The order of the cosmos is seven. The order of the cosmos is blue, perhaps yellow. That was the age of anxiety. Now we settle in for nerves. Neighbor girls trick-or-treat as loaded dice. The load: ghosts, orders, statistics, then the moon and unidentified objects in the sky. Now fried oysters and apple pie. This is not that artless time. Carrying some microorganism outa intagalactic space. He even thought the sentence resembled intestines. Otherwise he'd never wake up or take instructions in a dream. Otherwise he's just stuttering. And she was speaking about a box within a box in which a kiss was, and Napoleon would save the kiss from the kisser and the kissed. Chora. Squeaking with one voice, a forest of field mice. A mare and twin foal, here known as art and something else: trouble in Santa Fe. Main light, curved, cross-eyed. This is my red writing. She swallows her speech, she coughs often and sings. How can I keep a thought up? As in a love poem, from music slowing down, as if it were running out.

You have to sleep to have an unconscious; you have to hold hand with yourself to dream. I love to come into light. Its pool of heaven— a fish swimmeth therein. I am the fish in the pool of light, under the rock of heaven, coming out to meet the fathers. The Tanglewood Women's Forest will assist.

The Nocturnes. The nocturned are greasy (like morning light). You might climb a tree. You might meet a bear. You would learn a lesson. Your morality would improve. So you slip back and sweat. So the muscles green up and start to grow. If you can't keep'em, count'em: two, three, four, wah-doo, dee-dee, dee-dee. No eschaton, book without beginning or end, and you never find the passage you remember, never remember the passage you find. You can't keep it like sperm in a bank.

The Extravagant Scent Bottle. A smell of popcorn and the need to join vision to power attracted me to the palatial movie house where I watched the matinee. It was about a family of bears who moved to Scarsdale. My heart was warmed to see the citizens as they came to know and trust the bears. They learned to speak bear language and lick the children. With intense concentration I could see the images upside down. In the dark my fellows hung suspended. It is always four years to the Revolution, and it still was.

> Whomans
> in the whosmos — Fathers —
> a looseness of fit, your shirts
> the sleeves rolled
> to the elbow
> to fit at the wrists,
> and history is a leaky ball-point,
> fouling the pocket.
>
>
> People do not replace old dictionaries
> with pleasure (a known fact),
> and the Islamic court sentenced one whoman
> to two years for moaning
> with pleasure whilst fucking.
> The dictionary should be timeless.
> It should not moan with pleasure
> or be replaced.
> The Islamic court sentenced the dictionary
> to be timeless,
> disallowed western music,
> including moans of pleasure whilst fucking,
> and vat a musical idea constitutes?
>
>
> Isn't there any sugar?
> The father-image, sugar, becomes a permanent

axis of the child's development.
And it was said that Ludwig was the son of Friedrich
    Wilhelm II,
and it was said that he was the son of Frederick the Great,
and Ludwig vas loath to deny these rumors.
What does constitute a musical idea?

Dadaism (wasm) was born
the same year as my father,
across the street from Lenin's apartment.
There was a shortage of sugar for coffee,
there was a shortage of coffee.
Lenin had headaches from lack of coffee.
Kurt Schwitters' machine wrote symphonies
in the heroic style of Beethoven.
It may be found in an attic.
If there is confusion it will rise and fall,
because currents of still life run through the automaton,
because we have life but we are still not living,
because we own the mirror but not the image in it,
because life is deaf, like Beethoven,
and we keep our conversation books,
and write with clear firm hands,
and Beethoven, dada, is Zeus,
with thunder and storms,
and I have a sponge umbrella
and books which make me cough—their dust—
and books which make me cry
in the thunder (of the book),
because facial muscles, being small,
attached to mobile parts of the body,
respond to feeble waves of nervous excitement,
a gesture, a grimace, a movement of mimicry,
a movement, a shudder, nay—
an arrestation of habitual movement—
the physiognomy of the word,
the brow of Lenin's headache,
the leer of Beethoven's listening horn.

Friedrich Wilhelm II was Beethoven's father
and the King is dead (ole Zeus the king is dead,
and his image at Olympus
is near the whomus).
And again what constitutes a musical idea? its
valves and electrical systems, muscular walls,
an ordinary box which plays in forte-piano,
sublime hammer, and harp harmonique.
It moans with pleasure and sometimes
cries out: one of the boys said,
it was as big as a house,
one reported a throbbing (in sublime hammer),
another a hissing sound,
one saw animal eyes in a tree
(what he thought were animal eyes).
The company saw a figure, fifteen
feet tall, blood-red face, blond hair,
and glowing green-orange eyes.
Mrs. Hill thought she saw
clothing like folds, clothing like folds,
clothing like folds.
Moog tongued,
lipped lunged.
Dada was mistaken for a deity until he slept,
until he wept, until he spoke,
until a particularly calm
and meteorologically stable period in Danora, P.A.,
when air pollutants accumulated,
faire maydens were made captive,
questyng knichtes were turned to stone,
many people were hospitalized,
and twenty people died.
Ethylene Ethel drove her '36 Chevy coupe
straight to L.A. —natch—
an aura of ineffable vagueness
surrounds the term.

And Ethel is my mother
(she is your mother, gentle reader).

She pops the clutch, jabs
the accelerator. The father-to-be
would not be able to help his wife
during the pregnancy; he would not
see his baby for months or years,
if ever. Yet he was deeply happy
going off to war, feeling
his life would be continued.

The time is nigh when all whomans will be artists of desire. Commercial television approximates this condition. Market research allows the networks to present the average drama its audience requires. Television drama mixes the familiar and the new in a blend that is diverting and comfortable. It allows diversion up to but not beyond distress. The time is nigh when the audience will be able to program its own drama: video games are a step in this direction, so are video tapes. Video discs will make programming as much a matter of audience control as recorded music. The time is nigh when producers of personal computers will offer hard-and-software which will allow the opportunity for total self-expression. No inputs but taste will be required. Dreaming and day-dreaming will be replaced by computer synthesized display.

The video-image, father, is
the axis of the child's development.

                          The axle:
hands and arms cannot rotate perpetually,
fatigue prevents man from becoming a robot.
The clock makers contributed much
to the shape of the industrial revolution:
the shape of steam, the conversion
of the piston's reciprocating motion
into rotary motion,

                    rotary emotion,
romances, novels of family life.
Watt added a fly-ball governor;
Kay's flying shuttle

increased weaving speed,
freeing one hand for other tasks.
The flying shuttle required more yarn:
Hargreaves developed the spinning jenny
(named for his wife);
Cartwright developed his loom
to take up Hargreaves' excess.

Fatigue prevents whomans from becoming robots;
they have catheter ray tubes instead.
RCA reports a reading device built like
a frog's eye (in a frog's eye!),
layers of light sensitive photo cells,
like six layers of retina in Rana's apparatus.
Bell laboratories have developed a machine
to read handwriting. This capital we speak of?
call it ways and means, language,
habits and techniques, also tools,
loot from Spanish mines in Mexico and Peru,
the fertile, unpopulated earth of the western
hemisphere, slave trade,
opium, the conquest of India—
money used to underwrite empires,
equip trading expeditions,
open mines and manufacture armaments:
dark beginnings of the Age of Enlightenment,
unfettered interplay of avaricious instincts,
leading to stalemate. Everything
was being gobbled up
by everyone else.
Because Mr. Untermeyer and I
had gotten into a state—
a small state in Latin America,
bananas, a little coffee, prospects
of copper—where anything
he wanted to do (gobble, gobble)
I opposed in principle,
and everything I wanted to do he
opposed in principle—absolute

inaction on the Kreuger and Toll
side of the picture. We couldn't
get a trustee in bankruptcy,
couldn't get a successor trustee,
couldn't get representation on the Board
of Liquidators, couldn't get enough
deposits of bonds that we could speak
with authority. The History of Gestures
leaves no doubt: whomankind
progressively diminished
the uses of its extensions in space
as a means of communication
until the twentieth century,
when only the eyes and the bowels
moved, and mind crystallized,
as we demonstrated by applying
a faradic current
to the skin of an elderly man
whose face was analgesic
to stimulate each muscle group
separately and avoid all expression of pain.

Dactyl: literally finger,
from the fact the three syllables
have the longest one first,
as if writing poems
were picking posies,
and I've been whole,
playing a jew's harp
until my jaw's ached
                    THUwang THUwang
digadigadigadig.

Eras in English poetry,
ears in English poetry,
eyes, noses, and throats in English poetry,
but now we will feature the nose:

Originally a Persian flower the tulip
the tulip swear it the cause the first panic
panic capitalism Amsterdam 1637
the price of one bulb rose the tulip
50 to 1440 florins (flowers)—
some speculators started to sell no
Pan in the panic
greedic.
Compare now as escape with pride
so many die and come back
holding a greed flowers—
light because light is mind dark
until it strikes how or there
where vaudeville houses with hoofers
jugglers jug bands Mr. Wool
and Mr. Worth
impersonators

   Yass
give themselves
           THUwang THUwang
to full houses and the audience more
itself than the tragic man himself some other
deep inside whomic theaters impossible
to fulfill the deities did walk
and who sought them not—there—
sought them in the impossible light.

Frank Woolworth installed a pipe organ,
the dimestore, Fourteenth Street.
You hear Sousa,
always Sousa in the music box, the military band,
beer hall bands and symphony orchestras:
hide-bound musical bodies hemmed-in,
Sousa, laws
as unchanging as among the Medes
or the Persians.   Sousa,
Sousa, and Napoleon

on the laws of tragedy:
the hero must never eat on stage
or sleep;
            tragedy becomes comedy
when the hero sits. Thus Hemingway
wrote standing.

I am at my writing desk,
the tailor's posture.
And Nietzsche wrote to Jacob Burckhardt:
Condemned to entertain the next eternity
with bad jokes;
I have this writing business here.
(Frank Woolworth had a dimestore).

The tulip, originally a Persian flower—
cup-shaped (the cave, the life in it,
in your greed seized). Count'em:
six regular segments in two rows;
six free stamens, three-celled ovaries,
sessile stigma, ripening into leathery
many-seeded capsules. Crossed,
then double crossed, impossible
to refer plants to original types—
the cause the first panic—
their origins lost, their originality
worth premiums, Amsterdam.

This half-psychiatric musical excitement,
that metaphysical befogging:
unconscious prisoners of the frontier between
the possible and the impossible—half-psychiatric
musical excitement there;
ritual foundations;
economic style mystically bound and sacral—
magic until its subjects embrace animism.
In sunshine animists are active and merry,
in storms depressed,

and in long stretches of bad weather
run amok.
A man becomes a shaman through long-teaching,
his tongue is pierced, he fasts, he dresses
weirdly, he does not marry.
He expels evil power of malady,
mixes colors for painting,
composes sweet melody,
carrying the traffic of animistic cities—cities
in air, cities of air, and musical excitement,
biological bound and sacral growth
until animists embrace rationalism.

In the sunshine the rationalist is ironic and grave,
in storms willful, and in long stretches
of bad weather, he thinks and thinks
and sucks his teeth and thinks.
He becomes a philosopher through
long contemplation. He looks at a tree
and wonders, Is this a tree?
(a tree? a sign?) Yes,
yes, it is
a tree. He may marry
and procreate;
he is unable to expel
evil maladies, but he mixes
colors (Louis David said,
Let us grind red a-plenty,
heads a-plenty);
he composes melodies, but animals
do not follow him when he sings.
Psychiatric economic style logically
bound and sacral machines:
not people at first but distances
to be conquered:

    Phoenician merchants at Cadiz;
Arab merchants in Zanzibar from the eleventh century;

Chinese in the Indian Archipelago—
markets for gold dust, spices, pepper,
slaves, precious woods, and swallow nests.
Wasteland and woodland, swamp
and hill came under cultivation. The number
of glaciers and ice-flows increased;
winters became more severe; ice
covered the larger part of the earth.
And I still don't know if there were glaciers
in the Baltic,
when civilization dawned in Egypt—
the chariot drawn by geese—
or does it say teeth? Winters
became more severe: the little ice age
more a tyrant than the Sun King,
who wore a potato flower in his lapel,
whose chariot was drawn by smoke geese,
teeth, reason, an encyclopedia,
a calculus, stirrings
in the quilted coverlet.

The New World rustling its bed of corn shucks—
sweet smelling and troubled sleep;
banging drums and maize growing.
Maize virtually reproduced itself—irrigated
Andean terraces, lake sides of Mexican plateaux,
reproduces itself: thus,
Mayan pyramids, cyclopean walls of Cuzco,
Macchu Pichu thus, because maize virtually
reproduces itself. The New World spaces reproduce
themselves,
reproduce.

The biological *ancien régime*
shattered, stuttered:
births overbalanced deaths;
infant mortality dropped;
chronic famine, undernourishment
and virulent epidemics abated.

Between 1650 and 1850 the population doubled;
between 1850 and 1959 it doubled again;
and before the beginning of the third millennia....

    Takes a lot of voices
to sing a millennial song.

I'm telling a joke, I'm saying a prayer
(am I?). I'm going through the wilderness
of upstate New York. It's cold,
it's frozen the balls
off the pool table.
King Joe Bonaparte lives nearby,
and Frank Woolworth is born.
His brother Sumner said they'd stand mornings,
where the cows had lain to warm
their bare toes.
                  Frank took a job—
anything to get off the farm—
in a mercantile, Watertown.
He tried to play violin, flute.
When he opened his first store
the five-cent craze was on the decline.
The first days shinplasters—no nickels
in those days—an even nine bucks.
The failure, Utica,
seemed to him lack of variety;
his customers wanted variety. He added
Christmas ornaments and candy.
The public liked having its sweet tooth tickled.
He invested in a money bag
and advertised for a clerk. He opened
more stores, he added pocketbooks, suspenders,
belts: the answer was variety.

Meanwhile he travelled,
dropped into stores unannounced, and woe betides
the manager whose displays were slovenly.
The boss was ubiquitous.

You hear Sousa, Sousa,
raised in the shadow of the capitol's dome, Sousa
planned to run away with the circus—
he was enrolled in the Marine Band,
in the phonograph, in the hand
organ, music box, Sousa.
He wrote Dance Hilarious and With Pleasure,
which leaned Sousa toward the fox trot,
leaned Sousa, gave up dance music
and wrote war music during the war.
Free Lunch Cadets wrote Sousa
and Deed I has to Laugh for the minstrels,
for Carncross and Dixie maybe Sousa,
Sousa.

The Corsicans charged to the haunting shrill
of triton shells, not fifes and drums.
His name sounded Nabullione on the native tongues.
He liked black cherries,
he was not well hung,
he copied unfamiliar words in a notebook:
Dance of Daedalus
Pyrrhic dance
Odeum—theater—Prytaneum
Timandra, the courtezan who remained faithful
Rajahs
coconut milk
Lama
From Buffon he copied:
Some men are born with one testicle,
others have three.
They are stronger and more vigorous—
what a difference between an ox
and a bull.
He gave the Iron Cross
to Girolano Crescenti.
When critics murmured,
Giuseppini Grassini silenced them:
Crescenti's been wounded,

he was a castrato.
And under the Egyptian sky Napoleon
reminded his men that forty centuries
looked down upon them
from the pyramids, and the Russian sky
was empty even of birds,
as the Egyptian sky was full of history
The space made everything disappear,
even time itself. I've thought
so much about history that section
of my library is empty (worn away).
That wall of my study is gone.
Through the mortaged hole I see northern lights,
and the northern lights disappear,
or were never there in the first place.
My wife wears a perfume called Northern Lights.
Ornamentation of the body and decorative
mutilation appeared earlier than clothing.
Though all went naked, some
wore necklaces of bone, some tattooed
the most delicate flesh, some made-up
for man's defective speed and strength
with traps, namely deadfalls,
running nooses, and snares—nomadic
people who left through the library wall:
the pigmies of the Congo who build bridges,
the Eskimos who wall-up aging
parents in snow houses and leave them,
or pastoral nomads, tradesmen,
the Tatars sold Slavs as slaves
to Greek, Armenian, and Italian
middlemen who disposed of them
in Turkey and Syria.
Atilla extracted gifts from Byzantium.
The Tatar Nogay extracted gifts
from the Moscovites;
Bedouins of Arabia,
many Kirghiz, and Mongols of Asia,
many natives of southeastern Africa.
The Crow abandoned agriculture,

returned to nomadic life,
as did the Ostrogoths:
terror of evil eye, vampires, spells.
The dog howls, and a little drum is heard,
beaten by ghosts.

Sousa,
Sousa was to the march what
Strauss was to the waltz.
He shaved his beard,
thus defeating the Kaiser,
he wore new white gloves at every concert;
he was limp as a rag after *Siegfried*.
He beat time in circular motion. Sousa
mixed a salad, swept away dust,
and snatched Sousa, Sousa,
a butterfly from the bell of the contrabass.
He was the March King, April King.
When he wanted to write a march,
he turned his imagination to scenes
of barbaric splendor. Sousa.

And Frank Woolworth's automated organ
ground out some orchestral classic;
a portrait—Wagner or Beethoven,
Lizst or Mendelssohn—appeared on the wall,
listening, with allegorical background,
as painted by Joannes de Tahy.
Lightning crashed, when called for
by the music, thunder rolled,
rain descended. The newels
of the marble stairway, clothes closets,
and bed posts were piped for sound—
a lot of technology to play
a millennial song.
And I've seen
a mandolin movement in a musical snuff box—
a force field used to pucker

the skin of space, preparatory to passing
through the induced rent,
which heals behind the spaceship,
requiring a control loop of greater capacity,
greater than the proliferating variety.
When people change
their dwelling places,
they carry lighted brands,
a small blaze always burns
in cave or hut,
which may be made of grass,
branches of trees, leaves, reeds (including
bamboo). Sousa:

The Crusaders learned about barbaric
splendor and oriental luxuries: sugar cane,
candy, sherbet; they brought back
technologies and words: *barge, arsenal,
admiral, risk, magazine.* Europe
continued to feed on coarse soups
and gruels. At home they had the air
of being guests of themselves.

The scholars of the Sorbonne
prohibited rare beef and sexual intercourse
as causes of the Black Death.

Beatrice could hardly distinguish
between herself and others.

Byzantium was finally wiped out:
the Turks.

The learned Greeks
settled in Italy,
called a Renaissance.

And the Hundred Years War ended—the battle
of Chattilon—thus preserving the name
of the war.

Petrarch and Boccaccio sought ancient
manuscripts with pathos.

Leonardo
designed exquisite machines of terror.

And a class of Dionysiac merchants arose.
British landowners applied closure,
began to produce sheep—thus transforming
sheep into tigers. Hamburg introduced
fire insurance. The Fuggers produced tobacco,
had a salt monopoly,
exported opium from India to China,
imported wall paper, green tea,
Javan coffee, Malayan tin
(variety was important).
One Fugger brother refused to enter
the business,
saw the threat to his soul.

The dead were sewn in sacks,
buried in Clamart, sprinkled with quicklime.
The walls of the city were expanded,
in Ghent, Florence, and Strausbourg,
as often as required.
The mansard roof was a tax dodge.

Addison G. Jerome was the Napoleon
of the open board;
Daniel Drew; Jay Gould,
whose touch brought death, Jay Ghoul;
Corny Vanderbilt and his spiritualists,
Tennessee and Victoria Claftin,

who received oracles from Demosthenes;
Jubilee Jim Fish, born on April Fool's Day
(a joke on every one), and Black Friday Josie;
Russell Sage.
In time Black Friday and the Gold Ring
passed into legend. Ferdinand Ward,
the young Napoleon of Wall Street.
As the free silver campaign progressed,
all prophesied another period of panic:
prices fell, many new articles in tableware,
kitchen utensils, textiles,
came into Woolworth's price range.
Frank visited Napoleon's palace
in Compiègne, decided to have
an office like La Chambre Empire,
and he built a skyscraper cathedral
dimestore, which carried not a scrap
of indebtedness, his entirely,
erected on nickels and dimes:
to renew himself, to renew the people
by example, Confucius, Napoleon,
Frank Woolworth, who wanted
to sell a watch for a dime.

He asked for a spoonful of coffee
(Napoleon).
It was forbidden.
A little coffee forbidden,
he could have orange-flower water.
Please some coffee.
No orange-flower water or lemonade.
What is my son's name?
Napoleon.
Napoleon is dying.
Yes, you are dying. Your son is well.

Which is better?

Orange-flower water or lemonade?

Orange-flower water is heavy,
not so refreshing.
What do the doctors advise?
Whatever you fancy.
No, coffee is forbidden.
Lemonade is lighter.
Yes sir.
What is my son's name?
Napoleon.
I am dying.
Your son Napoleon is well.
He is not Emperor?

No sir.
Orange-flower water is made with barley?
No sir, almonds.
Is there a drink made with cherries.
Yes sir.
From apples?
Yes sir.
From pears?
No.
With almonds? Oh yes, Orange-flower water.
With walnuts.
No sir.
Walnuts grow in cold countries
and almonds in warm?
Yes sir.
Is there a drink made from cherries?

Dying, in his Napoleonic bed,
Frank Woolworth deplored
that America is not a musical nation
like Germany and Italy.

THE BOOK OF THE SUN,
THE BOOK OF MAN (COMPLETE)

For Charles Stein

*You can't hear God speak to someone else, you can hear
him only if you are being addressed. —That is a grammati-
cal remark.*

Things try to stand for other things,
and they do, after a fashion.
The computer stands for the Eye
of the Sun God. The set of all sets
is a set, but the set of all lions
is not a lion (stands for lions
after a fashion). If time were cyclic
and celestial motion limited
to perfect circles, if the twelve
constellations were evenly spaced
and the twelve moon months equal
to one solar year, then
the single-wheeled chariot of the Sun
would be the equal-tempered scale,
and this gerryrigged scheme,
after a fashion, has been
the private object. The square
root of a negative number—i,
it's called—turns up here and there
in the formulae, because the biped
is not a pure ratio
but a troublesome interval.
Having sneaked-up on himself from behind,
he thought he was someone else,
and he thought the circle he'd
sneaked around was cosmic space,
and he thought he thought
he thought was cosmic space was,
and his backyard became
toward the end of the sixth millennia
a suburban patio with a pic-
nic table and a bottle of beer,
unfathomable mysteries. So:

What can I know?

Clichéd chicken
and most potatoes
also peas

creamed
and how the chill knowledge is a ledge
more sentimental than velvet.
I come to the ledge and lose the distance,
a sense of the distance,
sentimental about sentences,
about human history and family life,
about listening to language untangle about
(therefore: the commune of light).
Are elms dust? crystal
butter dishes, beside the creamed peas.

And you can listen to music—
close, all day long:
a smell of eternity—
like dust, a circle,
a poetic calculus,
a geometry of intensified space use,
to increase profits by reducing size.

        WOOLWORTH
        INTENSIFIES
        SPACE USE

—what the newspaper says,
Medical Science (it says) the next twenty years
to unlock secrets of emortality,
SECRETS OF EMORTALITY,
the next thirty years (it says). The reading,
the reading of this book, gentle reader,
cures the gout and ringing in the ears;
it cures warts and premature ejaculation.
And how would you know
if the syllogistic engram
(about Socrates) were true?
The house you live in true?
The habit of it verified, if men are not?
mortal? will not be, when space use

intensifies,
until space is zero,
and profits? The intense mandolin playing
keeps coming, a kind of yeast,
goes straight to your head,
goes straight to your head,
behind your words and to the left,
in Broca's area, soak't up into music,
and changing clouds (of music) in the soaking
of the changing in the doing, the mandolin
and sublation in many stories,
mirrors, causing an upstate.
It's not easy to live in a place
named by relation to another
place: East St. Louis and almost St. Paul
share this fate with upstate New York.
Odd food, God Coffee—the sign said—
I've been looking for this diner—
East St. Louis—all my life. Imagine:
your brain the executive branch
of a large business. For Eccles,
god, mind, and free-will occur
in the synaptic clefts, like inter-office
memos and coffee.
When novel objects
occur in the synaptic cleft,
Freckles assumes a preferred posture
and freezes. Ice, cold winds, bad
roads into the hinterlands.
He may scream often,
he covers his eyes and turns his back.
Then he begins to jump up
and of course down. To jump
up only—this is god, mind—threatening
the novel object. Neurons fire
for no obvious reason;
the system is noisy. The brain
calls for a show of hands—
goes with the average, overcomes
the noise, until the average pedestrian

seems a guerilla in disguise,
a carrier of high velocity dynamite
and automatic weapons,
anthrax, pneumonic plague,
and average brucellosis. So:
this is the cosmos of strategic policy;
the naming of roses after presidents;
the naming of orchids after the breeders' wives.
In the deep recesses of military research
in the land of the Rockies and the Urals,
they seek the G answer—the means,
likely electromagnetic they think,
they think they think they think
of defying gravity and the proper
names of flowers,
the flow in the flowers.
So much noise for so much music,
a constant,
observed throughout the universe.

We had the International Greed party,
now we have the National Fear Party
again.   Dimetrius has freeze rays,
Anne has defrosting rays.   Dimetrius'
wild cats are with him.   Anne
has a panther.   Professor Dimetrius holds forth
on the nature of freezing rays
and disappearing rays, making a survey
of all gestural possibilities.   The power
consumed by the thinking brain is about
twenty watts.   Why is thinking so hard?
When you talk sounds run
out of your mouth like water
that overflows too full a basin.
It floods your body
on which it sprawls.
Each syllabical wave discharges
and unfurls itself on you
in an unconscious, unquestionable

manner.   Your body knows
how to note its progress, owing
to its cutaneous sensibility,
control of which operates like a keyboard,
responding to acoustic pressure,
freezing rays, the G-answer:
you've exhilarated right out of
cortical time, decomposing an opera,
a work not of art,
an act of hygiene:
the water organ of civilized life,
the watery organs or glass bells,
the visible body of language.

That the language is not optimal is a religious assertion. This is a
religious work. It's easier for me to (pause) stalk—talk staccato and
breaking up, up sentences into words, provided they have
(oh)(pause) not many syllables: ah! 'syllable' is hard. Precise words I
have trouble with are Republican and Epics—epis (pause) copalian.

The immune system begins to attack its host, functions of the
brain deteriorate, tissues cease transporting metabolites. Many cel-
lular enzymes turn heat sensitive, and you lapse into prose. When
you talk, sounds run out of your mouth like water that overflows too
full a basin. The bizarre excesses are right all tents of the itinerants.
The children are delighting and from entertaining. The swings and
arm chairs turn of an axis. Can you see the trailers come from gypsies
and acrobats? They go to the public work of the surfaces, and Dr.
Féré had a patient who laughed every time her carriage rolled over
the rough French pavé, its public surface. Waves related to what the
brain is doing and a small change in the mobility of electrons in
protein effects whole sheets. We laugh as we cross their surfaces.

And Dimetrius—another Dimetrius—
King of Macedonia, besieges Rhodes,
and the Rhodians not only talk,
those rhetoric teachers—but also endure:
when Dimetrius gives up the siege

and abandons the engines of war,
the Rhodians build Colossus
from scrap, war garbage (and
you can make no Image from a mushroom
cloud, but a mushroom cloud an image
of itself overflows too full a basin
or the basin itself overflows—
a toad-stool cloud).

Veniaminoff remembers everything.
The earth does not remember:
the mighty Rhodian image thrown-down,
after fifty-six years.
Veniaminoff writes down
what he wants to forget.
Colossus was shaken and dropped.
And Christian Hernaker talked
a few hours after his birth;
by fourteen months he'd memorized the Bible;
at three was studying ancient history,
Greek, geography;
died at four (worn-out).   The face
of the earth is a graveyard.

The nomads of the interior crowd
their great ranges as green as ever
until the dry years come: dust,
like the circle, a symbol
of eternity, and a hundred rabbits
eat as much as one cow.   How much
do three goats eat? do sheep?
To those who run the future,
there's always a better goat, a better
nerve gas, producing confusion,
narcosis, paralysis, blindness; some
incapacitate a foe by casting him
into a dream world of depression
or witless euphoria; mosquitoes
infested with yellow fever and malaria;

fleas infected with plague;
ticks with tularemia, relapsing
fever and Colorado fever;
horseflies with cholera and anthrax,
dysentery. They manipulate temperatures,
shooting material into the upper atmosphere,
thus lowering the temperature below;
interrupt the heat being radiated from earth,
thus raising the earth's temperature;
and set off explosions on the continental shelf,
causing tidal waves and earthquakes;
or target continents for catastrophic rains.

Los Angeles approaches San Francisco,
one foot every six years;
India heads north, buckling
and doubling back, creating the Himalayas,
compressing Tibet; China
edges eastward; the Ring of Fire
girdles the Pacific; the cities wave
like corn fields in the breeze;
houses seem to leap upward;
the earth opens and swallows forty horsemen,
whose cries are heard long after.

I play utterly abstract music
on a bass kazoo.

What ought,
what ought,
what ought I do?

And am I worth the guess
you make?

O fact
so
digga digga

digga digga digga
in circumstance
doing music
such as such, so:
gerry-
textually.

They're going to play *The Pines of Rome* (again),
and the glee club will sing.
They've got a brass
lad to play a French horn
or a harmonica who'd,
a glass oud,
or the disparity between naming objects
and using grammar.
It's always possible to add another axiom:
language use depends upon unboundedness—
precisions and peculiarities
I can hardly manage,
considering the delinquency of short-squirm
memory. I oughta
add another axiom.

Mt. Fuji has disappeared.
Is it still on the yen?
Some people can see only animate objects—
mules and daffodils—
others can see only inanimate objects.
The soul of the pin-ball
machine left the pin-ball machine
and entered the cocktail
waitress: WE MUST DO SOMETHING
(a French terrorist group).

The curse of the state in Europe
is its visibility;
here its curse is its invisibility:
a constitution,

a body (hidden),
a pornographic
self-help
book
with a Bill of Rights
and a mantle
of behavioral plasticity.

The poly-
syllables are here.
The body snatchers are vibrating
at our feet as if they were dancing,
as described in *Car and Driver*
a) the lesion or rupture,
b) the moment of giddiness,
and c) the provisional act
or a pine grove, swaying
like speech,
a grove of speech.
The nose is in low-
central position in lyric space
stretched through time,
including the unborn and the dead.
Listening to hear
the hearing,
the ears working,
little grunts as they strain.
I use words because they are so many,
so different, because I have to try
twice to say
some of them,
and between tries something happens
sometimes, which I elsewhere call
clinamen—a term, I think,
used by Lucretius—it means
swerve, I swear,
as described in *Car and Driver*,
and I think that's what I oughta do now:
add another axiom.

No depths correspond to these heights,
even theoretically. A mirror
is not so deep as it looks. The un-
conscious is the last refuse
of scoundrels, totalitarians,
and metaphysicians. Prisons and card
catalogs are metaphysical entities:
you and my jism
                    wasm
straight into the sky.

What would you say
to extraterrestrial beings? The chief
commodity of interstellar trade
(it says) will be information. We'll
get their poetry and music.
Perhaps this ball
of extraterrestial scum life
will be the size of a human head,
but evolved from unicellular
organisms, it would be a tribe
or nation, not an individual,
and its technology run wild?
Insane and cancerously
spreading,
decaying acoustico-gnostic systems,
disrupting inner-simultaneous speech schemata,
or verbo-motor ability sequences.
You also find ya'self
in interstellar space (information).

Let the prisoners of conscience go;
let the prisoners of consciousness go.

The twelve princesses
danced
wore-out their slippers

each night.
The king their father
locked their chambers.

They danced each night.
Somewhere they danced.
He posted watch.

Despotism begins
at home each night
they danced.

The philosopher failed
to explain.
Despotism

begins when the philosopher
explains
or fails to explain.

The necromancer failed
to explain.
The King offered

a choice of the daughters
to the hero
who would explain.

After three days and
failure always
was death.

Each third day
was a new hero
and the eldest

daughter gave him
drugged wine
before she retired.

He slept. They danced,
wore-out their slippers.
The hero died.

At last a young man
of no name
appeared,

and Death favored him,
telling him,
Drink not the wine,

and he honored
her wisdom
knowing no other.

When the princesses
went to the Cave
of Dancing,

he followed
and reported to the King
but was not believed.

On the second night
he followed
and danced himself

with the princesses
and reported to the King
and was not believed.

On the third night
he told the king
himself to follow,

and he did, seeing.
He offered the hero
his choice of the daughters,

and the young man said
they were unjust
cruel bitches all;

he'd have none of them;
he'd take his
chances with Death.

digga digga
digga digga digga.

I am writing something:
a poem brings the language with it.

I do not love the work of barbarism,
but I am called.

What can I hope for?

Nothing.

And what was man?

The weathercock fell from City Hall. The mayor was struck and
died by mid-morning. The bishop wrecked his Buick against the
shrine near the cathedral and died. Timmy The Stick P— was shot
in the head, at close range, as he ate breakfast at the Cafe N—. It

was the vernal equinox. The entire faculty of the university died in its sleep.

The painter left the opening of his show at a famous gallery with the heiress to a fast-chicken franchise. They were found, intertwined on a leopard-skin couch in her fashionable apartment, dead. The poet, reading a poem addressed to his mother, had a heart attack and died in the Library of Congress.

The newspaper did not appear. It was spring. The crocuses and the daffodils were in bloom.

He rose that morning filled with fear and hope. He thought to conquer death by dying, by ritual obsession and imitation of the inanimate.

He poached two eggs, fried two strips of bacon, and toasted two slices of bread. These he arranged on the platter thus:

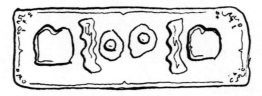

Then he thought better and arranged them in this fashion:

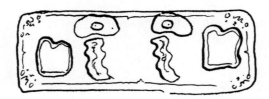

This satisfied him, and he ate. His appetite surprised him. He also ate a banana, making in sum seven items. He longed for a cup of coffee, which would make eight items in all (not a happy number). His unsatisfied desire for coffee began dialectically to call his satisfaction with representation into question, and the differences which appeared became the focus of his fear and hope.

He began to consider the proper names of these items. The eggs were Ester and Gladys, twins, from Iowa, where they had taken degrees in agricultural musicology at the State University. He was seldom frivolous with this activity, but the brightness of the spring morning was having a peculiar and happy effect on him.

He named musical notes, the colors of house plants, the echoes which could be heard from Ilene, at the head of the stairs and from Ernest, facing the dining room from the refrigerator.

He named the sounds which arose from the street (many of which never returned, to have their names confirmed), the slant of light through the bedroom window, which for a week around winter solstice reached the glass knob on the closet door, and the silence which ensued the toilet's flushing.

He did not name desires as desires but by the name of the place where he felt them. He had a desire for Ilene, so the desire and an echo were coincident, and the desire returned.

He was across words as he might be across a continent. This phenomenon was *known* as Lewis and Clark, though that was probably not its name. It might have been had things turned out differently for Meriweather Lewis, whose memory he loved and called Sacajawea.

The distance from his library window to the river was X13-31X, and he feared it—not as symmetrical as it appears, and it might cause floods. He had named it, as he had named his other fears, with the formulae of a mathematics the laws of which are unknown and unknowable. It could not be solved for him or he for it. His fear and its solution, therefore, were separated by an impenetrable barrier of ignorance.

His fear of the cul de sac at the end of his street was X7-7+semi— an anomaly on two counts, in containing elements which *appear* to be self-canceling and also an element which may not be strictly mathematical.

His I did not have a name. When the winds blew hard, he sat at the library window and named the forms which were taken by the leaves in the maple tree.

He was troubled by his own lack of a proper name, and many of his hopes were associated with this matter. The naming of hopes was problematic because if they were satisfied, they changed or disappeared, leaving certain items in the lexicon with the status of something like ghosts. And, of course, if these empty signs should accumulate, they would be extraordinarily difficult to keep track of. One of them might even come to stand undetected in an important formulation, and it would, therefore, be a formulation built on sand or worse than sand—in fact, nothing at all.

On the other hand, as hope intimately involved the problem of naming the I, he could not avoid the question. It became the object of obsessive conjecture, related—he discovered—to the matter of Ilene—an area at the head of the stairs, roughly defined by three threadbare spots on the rug. She began to take on considerable significance. He was a little giddy standing there, uncertain whether it was an aura or a return of the acrophobia which had inflicted him in his youth. He began to name places in relation to Ilene, rather than in relation to himself or the place itself. The corresponding area on the first floor, directly beneath Ilene, under the spiral stairs, he called anti-Ilene—a place, as far as he could tell, without qualities. The distance between it and Ilene was precisely $[x-1]$—the brackets indicating a potential, not an actual, fear. The corresponding area on the roof was super-Ilene, and his relationship to it was completely conjectural.

In time, he began to talk to Ilene. Pleasantries, at first. Good morning Ilene, did you sleep well? and so forth. But then he began to share his conjectures with her, and even to consult her about the uncertain names of things. About these matters she held definite opinions, but she usually deferred to him.

One night, after he had successfully named the relationship between the color of urine and protein (Charles-Alice, the first androgynous name), he could not sleep for considering the name of the triangle formed by T. Robert Pearce, where he slept, Anti-Ilene, and 7X3. He took his pillow and blanket (both unnamed) and carried them to Ilene, where he laid down with his head near her.

She advised him to sleep. It would be clearer in the morning.

He slept and dreamed of a chorus of voices—a voice something like Ilene's, the voice of an old man, and a voice with a foreign accent, perhaps Germans or Chinese—repeating the name Zotoz. It began to sound like the sea: Zotoz, Zotoz, Zotoz.

It's Zotoz, he said to her, when he woke in the morning. An odd name, she said. We have nothing like it, he said. Yes, said she, the names are beginning to get interesting.

During the following days he began to sleep regularly beside Ilene, and odd names became the norm: Yerbutu, Aaxle, Galalala. He wondered if these were his names or hers, but he was taking too much pleasure in her company, and he refused to pursue the question. His had been a lonely quest, and he began to think of, wonder if, she would want to enter into it fully—to become his partner, his mate.

She had begun in recent days to name parts of his body. True, they had had a spat when she insisted that his male parts had feminine names, but that had passed now and was on its way to becoming a joke between them.

His back had been bothering him for some days. Shooting pains would begin in his lower back or even his hips and extend up into his shoulders. They were uncertain what to call them, but it seemed certain that it was a result of his sleeping on Mootus-koono, his place on the hall floor, precisely the shape of his body.

To make a long story short—as it was much like many other stories which have been adequately told—they were married on the beautiful day the sky was a corpse. He named the distance from Ilene to his bed Ecstasia (yielding to the sentiment of the day), and he proposed by daily meditation to move Ilene along Ecstasia until her existence would manifest itself along that line continuously. He thought at first, if that feat could be achieved, he would gradually draw her in, and she along with it, but he realized that Ecstasia was properly a medium, and Ilene might be transmitted about the house. She might join him for breakfast or at the library window, to watch a storm. This would require some rearrangement of his mental furniture, but he thought with practice it would be possible.

When he became fluent in this language, he disappeared. Some say it was a discourse which required, on balance, incompletion—large spaces unexplored, unnamed, uncreated. Some same Ilene was his seestor or himself, or it was first incest and then ritual cannibalism.

Some say Ilene was a killer.

THE BOOK OF THE LIGHTHOUSE:
Variations on No Theme

The truly apocalyptic view of the world is that things do not repeat themselves.

The highest building in the world

The highest unbuilding in the world.
    the cause is avarice

the cause is
radio
activity
if it is, if
cause is
causes
cancer
radio's
activity

the liar's
paradox is
in effect
the higher
mathematic
nervous
the lower
not the earth
and not not
the earth
fishin'
fission
not the earth.

The rope
in the way of itself
is a knot.
You can always add
another axiom
It's possible
to change the rules
one at a time
or altogether
as you go
you go
altogether
with the rules changed
the rules change
and the knot
draws tight
r-r-r
tighter:

THE LAST DAY OF THE WAR:

From this gesture—call it the Truman chop—thus:
hands open before the chest, fingers extended
toward the audience, both hands almost reaching out,
as if to take an object the size of a head,
that's to be shaken by the force of the speech;
thus: downward, from mid-chest to waist.
One thinks more of throwing the object down
than of dropping. You begin to hear a voice.

And then the hands rise, dumb, from being speech.
The right hand touches the ear, cupping to hear a roar
half a world away, and the left, itself nearly useless,
pauses near the jutted chin. Hands and forearms
do not extend from shoulders—always the elbows
are near the ribs—for these are speeches made once
and not repeated. When the arms swing at the sides,
near the body, they reciprocate as from a crankshaft,
thence to the dinner table, and the right hand pauses
above the salad fork. Its trajectory from linen
to salad bowl leaves a trail of smoke,
but as the conversation is enlivened by the meal,
the right hand finding the membranes of cucumber crisp
and delicate, the left hand draws circles in air
between the jaw and the ajoining table setting
or rests on the table cloth beside smothered pork chops,
feels the rich vowels spill over the knuckles
and the heavy covered wood give way to flesh.

In the night, after the right hand has clasped
and unclasped, again and again, until the fingers
become birds ready to fly away with congratulations,
the arms beside the sleeping body in the warm bed
rise and fall, chopping into an argument with sleep.

I lay with a nipple in my mouth. The breast was
larger than my head. I'd rouse myself and suck in,

I'd wait and rouse myself and suck in. The milk
was sweet and warm:
I believed myself to be speaking.

I believe myself to be speaking,
speaking pages and not speaking
pages voices crises, thinking
meaning into words, even
in course of using them:
the Light House is not the sun,
the Light House is not the sun.
This is more emphatic than I can say:
this is not that. Repeating
the words for emphasis,
repeating the words insists
upon their meaning; repeating
the words to empty them,
so old governments
fall, and the laws of physical
nature change,
so Angels of Death are snarled
in old grammars and new grammars
have the lordly virtue of accuracy:

this (remember) is advertising copy
(the liar's paradox is always in effect)—
a hundred volumes, in folio, unwritten,
are to follow.
It may be lies.
The world is constructed
to see itself,
but to do so, it cuts itself
up—blades, straight razors,
even blunt axes—
into states which see
and states which are seen:
the Light House confounded with sun,
the great Sign floats, unanchored,
like language, like a small boat,

where we are speaking (we believe),
raising death's heads in our sentences
and going westward. Still
takes a lot of voices
to sing a millennial song. Every ground
is sacred feeds us; every lake
sacred gives us sweet water.
Having raised great stones
to the Dead, we came in small,
stinking boats, sweating,
eyes sweat-full and bleary,
to lead splendor forth,
to enlighten accident,
raising death's heads in our sentences.

the Priestesses of the sun,
bare from the waists, sayeth *You humans*
fashion Images in Death's House—
And we killed them.
There was gold in their temples.
Thus we sang:
The light from the tower lights our way,
lightens our hearts.
There was gold in their temples,
you understand,
to stand for all things,
and gold light on the hills
beyond the temples.
We know our way home—the lighthouse,
the sun, the meta-
phors—our poets raise their voices,
and we know our way:

                    1. All is One.

                    2. All is One.

These were our tenets, like tents
we carried and songs we hummed

against heroic darkness.
We know our way back,
turning back, eyes over our shoulders.
Purple dawn, for nobility;
gold on the water.
What other metal is like it?
The color of the Tower's light,
light itself, gold,
gold on temple walls.

And rot did not take her,
the chief of them,
though she did not stir or breathe.
Her wounds healed,
and we were worried.
Flanks of such fineness,
blue-veined and cool,
and gold light about her; her hands
disappeared in her hair;
anemones, roses, centauries
grew from her mouth.
The smells of pine and cedar
were about her. We were worried,
and wrens were busy
in the pine trees.

Her eyelids blue veined
and gold light where scrub grew
in hills of chert and limestone,
where wolves ran, yellow-eyed, feeding
on abundant deer. Snowy owls
flew in the night and bear
and bad dreams troubled our sleep.
We woke coughing, unable to breathe,
the air was rich and treacherous
with the scent of wisteria.
We could not sleep:
the veins in her feet were blue.
The necromancers could not sleep:

one followed a raccoon,
the other porcupine.
Signs were various: meteors,
bird tracks in the sand,
large birds and portentous.
We slept on golden pillows
and had bad dreams.
The tuft of hair at her gate
was of such fineness,
and when we touched her,
she rose but not as one from sleep,
not bleary and uncertain.
Her voice was quick
and her gestures sublime.
It was not what she said
(which might have been anything),
but the way she said it,
and she said:
It might have been anything—
a thousand times and ways.
She said: *Giant cities stand empty*
and small populations huddle in their stone masses
as Stone Age peoples sheltered in caves.
She said, *The Universe cannot be distinguished*
from how you act upon it.
She said, *Do something;*
the gods are bored with your devotions.

COMPLETE STOP

Jamais vu:
I've never seen this before.
The cosmos of repetition
always belonged to someone else
(possibly a committee).
And how do you make a robot
more than an adding machine?
Supply it with philosophy,

preferably one expressed as a riff
to improvise on.
                  I'll write it up.
I am at home and not at home.
You can tell: the liar's paradox
is in effect. The music
(the lyre) divided into parts:
by Wednesday it sounded like sand
blown against plate glass.
I am going to speak
and then not to speak
and in the space between these events
it will rain:

I ANNOUNCE THE END OF HUMAN MINDEDNESS.
COMPLETE STOP

And something else begins,
something else now:
the civil war begins again
(to be done right this time) in caves
the Dordogne, Kentucky, the Ozarks,
cliffs of Africa and New Mexico,
or hotels, New Orleans, with cajun music
and food in the air—*Jour Ouvert*—
the Mardi Gras, the Civil War begin.
And no one knows who's
black and who's white.
You can't tell
by looking: the ego's
not found in separate bodies
anymore. Any body,
walking with its hands in its pockets
is liable to be shot on sight
(might have a grenade
or harmonica), and the Ghost Dancers
speculate on creating new need
in others to drive them, drive them.

The need industry drives them.
And the Civil War begins:
the art of destroying permanent symbols
does produce its own symbolism.
The ghosts of many white men
and many white women scream
when you touch a book,
and thine eyes canst not tell
black from white.
                              Time
works on the guerilla's side.
He does not try to hold
a territory. With a pistol
or a machete he can capture
a rifle (a saxophone). With twenty rifles,
he can capture a military patrol
or destroy a convoy that carries five
machines guns and fifty-thousand rounds.

He does not fight to control a territory,
but to win the minds of the population.
The Body Dancers beat out rhythms
on the drums with their feet. The drummers
reply and a competition develops.
The Jobo have talking xylophones.
Their players sit in the market
and comment on the events of the day.
The Ibo speak with flutes.
Cootie Williams mutes his trumpet
with a plumber's friend
and speaks. Becoming is the how-squared
of Being. Defining oneself is equivalent
in visual art to making oneself visible.
The Body Dancers withdraw
into jungles of indefinition
and regard the Infinite as polluting,
regard the whiteness of the the sky
with suspicion and parody Cronean rites
(Ghost Dancers repeating events

of the dream-time and becoming visible,
repeating playing dying in time,
out to eternity),
but dream is a fire burning alone,
out of contact with the common fire.

The common fire,
whence Buddy Bolden
arrives, cornet in hand—
Body Dancers of Storyville at his command.
I believe myself to be speaking,
speaking and rising, singing
and pointing. I believe myself
in the liar's paradox, where I meet
Buddy Bolden (who listens to himself,
as I listen to myself, and change
what I say when I've heard
what I've said).
Buddy Bolden went,
went to, want to—he was not prepared
to solve the complexities
of the musical world he'd opened.
Someone put something
in the mouth piece of his cornet
(voodoo), Kid Ory said;
one of his women removed
the bow from the sweat band
of Bolden's hat (voodoo): the funky
butt demons chased round
and round, no way
to get out of Bolden's hat—
measurable and repetitive. Buddy
entered a fan of time: paranoid
delusions, also grandiose.
Talks to self. Hears voices.
Picks things off walls. Hears
the voices, talks to self:
complexities of the musical world.
He insists on touching each post

in the ward and is not satisfied
until this task is accomplished.

We have limited possibilities:
the development of one aspect
of language brings the weakening of another.
Harmonic developments diminish possibilities
of melodic and rhythmic relations:
the logic of unending travel.
The Nilgari antelope pregnant
with an elephant may represent a myth
or a sense of humor.
But not both?

COMPLETE STOP

Q.   Why does the elephant write history?
A.   In order to forget.

STOP AGAIN

and count to eight.

We have limited possibilities: trying
to fix the grammar up,
the grammar up,
trying to climb up a rope up
we stretch as we climb,
carrying a bag of oranges,
bursting, grammar up:
entropy is creation,
and the grammar more powerful
to keep it together—a gateway
to musical madness, closed—
howdy-doo and opened, Buddy Bolden,
just a crack

digga
    diggadigga
diggadiggadiggadigga.

The greater voodoos first
synthesized urea, now they will
synthesize life itself—
as if there weren't piss
and life enough.
We have not found an adequate
substitute for the Oedipus complex.
I believe myself to be speaking.
I believe the cosmos is running
back the grammar up.
I believe it is possible to build
a light house. I've written it down.
I mean in time to forget.
I've written it down seven times
and left. I've written it out.
I mean in time to forget.
I've written it out
again. Thousands of learned
papers are published each year.
It's now easier to rediscover a fact
than to determine if someone else
has discovered it. This
is the boundary of the formèd cosmos—
Re's jism
    wasm
        anyway, come—
and we're beyond it.

The Information Theorists first said,
the more entropy the more information,
then they said the opposite.
They do not swing; their bodies
betray them. Is information choice
or determination?

The weatherman
reports the news before it happens;
other forms of journalism are inadequate.
The Truth is rumors
which pass through language
as weather passes through the sky,
after the fashion of dreams (somewhat),
but the structure is different,
and the content is different.
I am awake; I am doing it,
not having it done to me:
I mean, what I say to you,
and you say her,
and she says to them.
The World is a collection and. And.

One kind of sentence seems to stop,
another kind seems to go on.
The grammar of these forms
has been heard but not described.
In the beginning was a sentence (at least)
of the kind that goes on, and probably
many paragraphs, hanging together
like ill-fitting clothes
but serviceable enough.

That is, if it gets warm you can take
the jacket off, but not politely
in certain company. It's always
possible to say more than you intend
but not the reverse. I write
not for the; I write who
for this. I write not who out
of not night and who day.
I write one for it and thing
for soul. After practice,
this seems correct: the rocking
chair in the still life—

the cannibalism of style.
In the still life the orange
does not sit on the table.
I thought this incompetent
draftsmanship. Now I think
it represents a metaphysical truth.
For know I write now;
for then I write
observe the orange.

And a tornado watch is in effect
and will be until 2 a.m.
We watch by Oz light.
Everything is distinct:
I see every stalk of wheat,
the shasta daisies are in bloom.
The air conditioner (as I watch)
is a boat carrying me further
into the disaster of sleep.
Narratives appear,
like banks of ominous clouds.
They are the point and not the point.
I underestimated the sense of smell.
I overestimated the sense of well-being.
Everything is less necessary than it seems:

    I was in the swimming pool, the Ramada Inn, Santa Fe, talking to
the author of *The Last Seven Years on Earth*. He was from Tulsa on
earth. He had rented a condo, out in the mountains, with an option
to buy, didn't think he'd buy: no swimming pool. And he told me
about his new book *The Capstone of Existence*. He'd figured it out (or if
I understood aright he claimed divine guidance): as we know, Adam
was created in 4004 B.C. You see, Adam had a private object—those
other characters who painted the caves and left their bones all over
the place didn't. Well, Eve got to screwing around and got herself
knocked-up by one of these soulless bipeds. So it turns out, original
sin is genetic. I suggested we get the DNA splicers to work on it, but
he opined, Ye must be born again. He did, he said, Ye.

There *was* a rainbow over the roller disco, Santa Fe, the evening after I received this revelation—I got a picture of it—and another two days later, the most spectacular I've ever seen, as we drove east on I-44 toward Tucumcari.

This leaves some questions unanswered.

      That the world should exist?
and have meaning *too*?

How long does it take for an information cancer
to pass through a population?

I've become too abstract—
i.e. in too big a hurry. The hot-dog
stands at the apocalypse, the souvenir
shoppes (the Four Horsemen
for $4.99—about a buck-and-a-quarter
a head). The poem
is as long as its intention. The end's
as arbitrary as the beginning as.
I've lived a million years,
and I always will.
Have. Do. I went through
all the dead languages, first Greek
and Latin, then the others,
as were deader, taking trophies—
more than I could carry [home?],
and pre-Incan surgeons performed
successful trepannings,
some skulls neatly opened,
some just bashed in.
If brain capacity was declining,
they may have wondered
why their memories were failing,
why they were unable to carry out
mathematical calculations
with their former precisions, or why

they were subject to headaches
and tumors.

Were they trying to find out
what was going on,
to remove the tumor
or private object?

The experience of withdrawal
from a potent addictive drug: the fiend
chews his ear lobes in hope of relief
and listens to music from New Orleans.
I feel strange inside music from New Orleans.
I have feelings inside
I do not recognize as mine music
from New Orleans, and outside
I hear windows breaking
and home-made pipe bombs I hear.
I chew my earlobes
until tears come to my eyes
and tears (pronounced tares)
come to my eyes, and I hear the music
deep inside New Orleans,
Chicago, and KayCee. That is,
the musicians moved north
to find work. King Oliver
called up a young cornet player
by the name of Armstrong.
who later joined forces with Fatha Hines
and together they made some recordings
(about 1928 or 29) demonstrating
the information cancer had passed,
and then a clarinet player,
name of Teschemacher heard,
and passed the word,
but Frank Teschemacher died young.
His high school pals (those Chicago
swing types) cashed in. What'dya expect?
it was the depression.

Whereas in Kaycee Pendergast
kept people working—Harry Truman
and the musicians from the territories.
Ernest Hemingway worked for *The Star*,
compared the city to Rome—
the Seven Hills and so forth:
goes to show how political corruption
stems depression and creates culture.
And Ben Webster came 4 a.m.
to Mary Lou Williams' house.
Ben, Coleman Hawkins, Hershel
Evans, and Lester Young were jamming,
the Cherry Blossom Club,
and had worn out the piano player.
Would Mary Lou come and play?
The act of destroying permanent symbolism
does produce symbolism of it own.
London Bridge is in Arizona,
falling down, and the Piri Reis map
shows *someone* charted the coastline
of Antarctica some time before
the current glaciation.

Lester Young took pains to relax.
Swing: some combination of relaxation
and imminence of war. It was
the Kansas City bands that learned
to do head arrangements, head
rearrangements—Bennie Moten,
Andy Kirk and the Clouds of Joy,
the bands from the territories and Count Basie—
variations on no theme,
finally,
the jam sessions
and then the boppers, the Shakespearean
aspect of this music,
admitting the grotesque
alongside the sublime.

How many bands drove
two-hundred miles, five-
hundred miles, to learn
the dance was next week
or last night—broke
in Texarkana or Bartlesville.
The Anti-Christ has come, and
it has not come. Some
say it came secretly,
as to the door of a buffet flat,
where in an absolute sense he
was at her pleasure, hanging
from her brass-studded garter belt,
and she put Polish mustard
on her body, and he licked it
off, and he kissed her toes
and some say the Anti-Christ came
secretly, and some say he has not
come, and he kissed her toes—
first those on her right foot
and then those on her left,
uncertain which might give
the most pleasure, the left toes
connected to the right brain,
and the right toes connected
to the left brain, and he kissed up
her calves and into the hollow
behind her knees, first one
and then the other, working
toward the resolution of this
dilemma, and he slowly licked
along the backs of her thighs
and ran his nose around
the outsides of the labial folds.
He took first one labium
and then the other in his lips
and pushed them apart
by running his tongue along their inner-
sides, and here the dialectical uncertainties
were sublated. Some say the Anti-Christ

came. The clitoris was
hard and tasty and to it
he devoted his undivided attention.
And she had not been a passive
field on which these metaphysical
events transpired, and now,
swaying above him she imparted
the rhythm of the music to the shaft
of his penis, as she pushed back
the foreskin with a quick
circular movement of her tongue.

And it is to the symmetry
of this arrangement
that I call your attention.
She is language
and he the earth
or the reverse.
We'll never know for sure
who is speaking.

It will provide a climax for the poem, but I will leave it, as it were,
off-stage, like death in Greek tragedy. This is not ungenerous. If she
should pass a mouthful of warm seed to him, and he should work it
gently into her vagina with his tongue, reproduction would be that
much more like speech. Such confidence is possible only in times of
supreme historic clarity. The world exists and it does not exist. I am
not equivocating.

Charlie Parker accents on the beats
and between the beats. His phrase
contains notes that are not played
but only suggested—the bop microbe,
new riffs on chord changes
in familiar tunes, with many notes
not played but heard.
How many permutations were turned

on *I Got Rhythm*,
and Kenny Clarke playing rhythms
it'd take five feet to dance to.
Confirmation is
I Got Rhythm, Donna Lee
is *Indiana* and *Scrapple*
from the Apple is *Honeysuckle*
Rose. Groovin' High
is *Whisperin'*. *Ornithology* is
How High the Moon, and *Hot House*
is *What is This Thing Called Love?*
Anthropology is *I Got Rhythm*.
And then John Coltrane playing,
multi-voicing, stacking new chords
on top of old chords, playing
notes Bird only suggested,
and Ornette Coleman abandoned
harmony altogether.

It's appropriate it should come to an end as I listen to Beethoven
(thinking of Coleman)—a trio now, not one of the big gut-busters;
western civilization is over.

I did not chose to be a barbarian, but I have some talent for it.

The laughing biped's organism consists of a coil of light, like
coiled rope, and the end of the rope is somewhere about the belly
button. Sometimes the rope is unraveled and carried across a
thousand years when it is put back together, and though it is unravel-
ing and re-raveling in time, it is always existing and not existing.

A new person is proposed
or coming forth
without proposition,
and these people who move
and do what they do
as living while dying
arrive. They wear
neat ties, subtle

stripes. Their mouths
are okay—they consume—
but their eyes are blear
and rare (it's meat's
the metaphor).
They are people
in dread of themselves,
integrated circuits
developed in
space programs,
used in discos:
NASA to Studio 54.
It's party time in the USA.
PARTY TIME
and everyone is invited.

The theme of the party is
THE END OF THE WORLD:
you go right in
and you go right out—
the only absolute
kick in town.

Where is song
being placed ?
What does song
cut into?
He explodes (like a fire) into song.
A gber imo wang wang:
he sings clearly, brightly
(and we know *The Wang, Wang Blues*).
And *wang* in body, as in song:
to glisten or shine with palm oil,
castor oil, vaseline.
A wanger yum: like the headlights of a car.
And *i wanger*: as may be said of the day,
an idea, a kerosene lamp.
Those who glow with human fat
are irresistable,

and human fat merchants,
marked by a piece of a certain grass,
hanging from their lips,
come with sacks on their backs
and sit in a corner on the market.
You feel it
long before you hear it,
a throbbing beat, pulsing the floor and air,
pushed through a forest of loud speakers.
Light shapes swim out of the dark.
They flash and spiral,
repeat themselves in mirrors;
revolving wheels of tinted light splash
the room with color,
a thousand facets of spinning mirror globes
fracture the light beams.
Discos in renovated lofts
and machine shops,
in former taverns and converted theaters.
There's a disco in a soap factory
and an old Savings and Loan.
Disco lights are harsh.

THE NATURAL LOOK IS PASTY ON
THE DANCE FLOOR

1. Exaggerate
Heavy mascara is necessary under strobes

2. Define
Outline your lips with brown-bone crayon
then apply a heavy coating of lipstick

3. Reconstruct
Reshape your face, your cheek bones
and your chin with dark base.

It is two o'clock in the morning,
and the disco has become a steamy underworld
of leaping figures, swirling and spinning
in a kaleidoscope of revolving lights
which ricochet off mirrored walls and mirrored balls,
drench the parquet floor with pools
of light and puddles of color.
We have been dancing since midnight,
and body temperatures have been rising;
my husband's necktie was the first thing
to come off. I am wearing it as a sash.

The deejay once more nudges
the turntable to a faster pace
and higher pitch,
mixing record after record
so that each is a little faster,
higher in pitch and more intense,
urging the dancers toward frenzy.
Cries and calls and a thousand arms waving
fill the air as the music lifts the dancers
off their feet and off the floor
(the word in roller disco is flying).
The beat goes on, harder, faster,
crazier, and all at once fountains of smoke
pour from ceilings and a misty fog begins
to rise from the floor (cyanide gas).
I think of being able to take off my skin
and dance around in my bones.
The word for this feeling in roller disco
is flying.

COMPLETE STOP.

Disco dancers strobe-stopped
in the posture of flight.

FADE.

I'm hungry
more or less
always now.
I'm in the attitude
of receptivity
or consumption.
One way to deal
with the hunger
is to use
the hunger itself,
as material,
to make of the hunger
the thing
required
for its satisfaction.
The hermetic closure
of this productivity
might be overcome
with valves
or banks of light
emitting diodes
behind the eyes.
I make these things
to look like poems,
might have been
called poems
once,
and I open
the valve
between my nose
and chin.
The thing
escapes
one word
at a time
into the air.
I am going to
talk to you.
The street light
blinks

from red to green.
Signs are re-
choiring
my attention,
and I give it,
gladly,
as the rain
talks,
and I listen.
Everywhere wants me
to read it
and I do:
the limber trees
sway and speak;
Keith Kellogg
of Battle Creek
believed ham
and eggs
stimulated
erotic feelings,
and he man-
ufactured
cold cereals
so the young
would not
fall prey
to lust
and self
pollution;
the patron
of the pet shop
says, No,
I don't want
the puppy;
I just want
its life.

I want to say
I am my pasty

face.
You'll see
this life
inside it
inside
out it,
music?
Compooter
moo-sic
outside
breaking windows,
Jack,
and my face
opens
from a slit
(horizontal)
about a quarter
of the way up
from the chin
to the hair line,
the eyebrows
rise,
the eyes are wide,
and, and, and the filose chronicle:

In Newtonian times still to slink up
a body of light colors, pulses,
the vivid tree shakes and misremembers
its own sigh suits to a tee
the town's pastoral sight and you laugh
grief, grasp, municipal intelligence,
last leaves and fast falls bright exudations.

Insurgencies of pelagic land
script indecipherable hands, thick
and work-hardened on leisure air:
counterfeit diagrams of her melodies arise—
epistemic juke boxes slugged to postwar
nervous fingers pecking by the coffee mugs.

Their stainless steel faces shine—
I am five, misshapen by this music,
mistaken, thick bodied, and primed
nerve-endings to night sounds of semis
whining rubber and double-clutching on hills.

The bells of tills and churches ring,
mechanic castanets, which gears mesh—
sausage sellers of art and arms,
a second little world and a third,
each cloven from the prior Imago,
even miniature jack handles to fit
the miniature jacks, miniature meat and light.
The chemic burgers are bleached and dry
and then a green sunset in a purple haze.
Twisted inhabitants of order my love
wreathe the children's heads with light
and breathe the vapors from their eyes.

O denizens of the tree, events there,
unkempt resplendent verb things, light
red light in a ruby stone
and the spreading wake of the laser field.
The coherencies of my eye beam
broken and revealing a comatose keep of souls,
a little bowl of rude clay, seen close up,
as a great ship we disembark,
gesticulating and gibbering, totter
across space and fall from the world.

Edisonian clock-time processes,
Institute of Technology artists, trained
subtle arms makers rife, advertisers,
cancer-makers. I strode into her lair—
false bitch of generation, her thighs
blood-covered, blackening to the knees,
where pups fed on birth gore,
and her eyes keen to production, shit,

mucous, pups, ideas, lies, little boys,
books of wisdom. I strode into her lair,
thanked her goats and rubbed her belly—
jungle counting and riparian dreams
more than the sauces of ancient belief,
such twistiness and imperiousness of time.

The dead of a murderous nation, banging on dish pans
and carrying baskets of rutabagas
further into the lethargic kingdoms of tree, ice, stone,
where thought is not homocide
and symmetry not the sad tyrannic urge
of nervous, weak, war-mongering old politicians.
I am absorbed in watching the dead.
It is the watch, not I, which is ticking:
they move in one direction until a bell rings,
it may be a bell in their pockets
or hanging from their necks by chains—
they are so tangled in themselves—
a placement of vowels and consonants across a page—
in their sleep two notes clang in confusion
and seek the counsel of a third,
such keening dissonance and bell ringing
and with each tolling of the bell they turn,
resembling makers of verse,
wearing ruts in the heart's soft stone.
They adhere to our minds
and it is they in us who grieve,
counting and shouting their disbelief.

The shell fishes and tender shoots
of vegetable matter resembling speech
colonize the cave, following American policy,
and now threaten to declare themselves
in wise-ass remarks. We have entered
the celestial cave. You can hum along
if you don't know the words.
This is the peculiar dream space:
the goats are bigger or smaller

depending on their horsepower, their
spiritual condition, their love for you.
The institutional paths are strewn
with civilization and other enchantments,
where I find one day but not the others.
Cut glass of the cave's kaleidoscope
prisms glazed Buddha's and maji's journey.
A year's measure: yellow leaf,
red leaf with green veins,
blood leaf with white spots,
in the stroboscopic pleasure dome,
plumb apples and bright eyes,
warm thighs and spiritual revelations.

Untwistiness is also necessary:
your hands wrung out
and hung up to dry. The Australian figure,
who should have no name, talked too much
and made objects come into the world.
These Australians already had more objects
than they could carry over the rough bush and heat.
They didn't even want another hat.
So they took his mouth away,
and his silence was a blessing,
a blessing, a lesson, a true sentence.
I sat on a stump and prayed
for mystical substance to make a box,
to put things in and make them quiet,
light, noun-doings tape hiss
into histories nameless extravagance.

Angles of incidence, love's confusions
come to me with hands full time's pulse
come to me, counting out
loud parties.

　　　　Electioneering not allowed nearer paradise
than near a sign, bearing inscriptions,

counting out the time out the count:
a design cut in time.
Time has stood still—
if only it could.
Fadeless in the lapse of time.

The children absorb the data in the lap of time
and enter love's confusion:
the absolute quantity of child self,
the difference of love.
Outing the time itself out the count,
the ratio of grammar to rime,
objet d'art wrapped in velvet
to hand saw singing, basketball
dribbling, bird song.
The time counting itself out the count.
The nature of time and a chickadee
trade places;
the chickadee trades places with rules of thumb,
governing spiritual welfare,
its cadence without shadows.
The rules of thumb become suns,
the rules moving so their oppositions
light every cranny. The unconscious mind
the invisible army of Napoleon's century,
affronting time in Egypt, space in Russia,
beauty in Bayreuth, the darkness
Freud named in fear
sang out from hidden places
its dark ungrammatical sayings.

I am thinking
the wilderness of this name,
that it is time, and I never leave
and never find my way.
I meet with beings here and there,
who bring the lethargies of love and war,
bird watchers, bookmakers,

speculators in futures,
and the nature of these beings is to behave
in the electronic fashion—
to be here or there but not
between. Counting time is like counting
money in your pocket,
when you're down to your last dime:
one and not-one
but not zero and two.
When you are not counting you are not counting;
when you count you count
shhhhh one   shhhh one   shhhh one.

When I go
where I cannot see myself,
with a black jack staff and a blind dog,
the gelatinous goo and gewgaws of darkness
without measure gather
in veins and night bodies,
loathing pulses, a counting
empty as primitive time,
turning to expire again.

And a mad cricket sings:

    I come for your body your body
        my god's goodly bone house
        carved hieroglyph bone pillars in rib church
        cricket wisdom's tractates and bibelot
        where I lay me down
    with the cricket wife
        outside of time
        conceiving phonemes
        in the names of the cricket gods
        i k t c and so forth

    cricket song rules
    I am solipsism's cricket eye

song rules
obedience to song rules
and cricket affliction relieved.

I am a cricket asleep on a limb
above an empty ocean
deep waves in empty ocean
thought in empty mind's reflections
a wave, an impulse of music
I am heard, counting
in the hours called
the music continues
after the senseless slaughters
the haunting light of Rhodes
ghosts
living and repairing the Tower.

DON BYRD lives in Albany, New York, near the New York State Capitol, and is Professor of English at SUNY Albany. His published works include *Aesop's Garden, Charles Olson's Maximus, Technics of Travel,* and *The Poetics of the Common Knowledge.* He is writing a book-length essay entitled "Abstraction: The Cartoon." His recent poetry is "illiterate," recorded as audio files directly to a hard drive and edited and re-mixed digitally. Accordingly he has commented that "the alphabet is nearing the end of its usefulness."